GETTING SMARTER

The Study Skills Improvement Program

by Lawrence J. Greene and
Leigh Jones-Bamman

Fearon Education
Belmont, California

Simon & Schuster Supplementary Education Group

Acknowledgment:
    The authors would like to thank the following people for their contributions and support: Judith Brand, Dr. Henry Bamman, and Richard Jones-Bamman.

ISBN–0–8224–3386–9
Printed in the United States of America
1 . 9 8 7

Contents

A Message to Students

Being intelligent is not the same as being smart. You may ask yourself, "How can a person be intelligent and not be smart?" Well, being smart requires more than intelligence. Being smart involves being practical and having common sense, too. Being intelligent may be knowing a lot of facts that will help to answer homework questions, but being smart is remembering to take home the books you need to do the homework. Being smart is knowing *what* to study for an exam and knowing *how* to study for that exam efficiently. Being smart is figuring out how to complete a long assignment within a reasonable amount of time and do a good job on it without having to give up large parts of your life.

No matter how intelligent you are, *Getting Smarter* can make your life easier. This book will teach you a way to organize yourself and the material you are reading or studying. As you learn these skills, your school work will become easier, and your grades should improve.

There is no big mystery to academic achievement. The formula is simple:

$$\text{Skills} + \text{Effort} = \text{Achievement}$$

Getting Smarter is a study skills system designed to teach you how to function more efficiently in school. The step-by-step activities and exercises will clearly show you

- how to evaluate your current study habits
- how to become organized
- how to budget time
- how to establish priorities and goals
- how to improve study habits
- how to read with comprehension
- how to take notes
- how to take tests with better results

Although we have made every effort to make the process of becoming a better student as interesting and enjoyable as possible, learning better methods of studying demands personal effort. There is no magic potion that can transform you into a more efficient student. Study skills can be improved only by your own conscientious effort. The study skills that you are about to learn can be mastered quickly. Within a few days, you should be able to use your new study and organizational skills in school and at home.

The chapters in *Getting Smarter* are short enough so that you should be able to complete each one in thirty to ninety minutes. If you are willing to commit yourself to ten to fifteen hours of conscientious effort, then you can easily master the study skills that are presented in this book. These thoroughly proven, step-by-step methods will help you develop the organizational and analytical skills that are essential to your success in school. You will learn how to establish goals and priorities, how to organize and remember information, and how to study efficiently. *Getting Smarter* is a practical book that shows you how to become academically confident and competent.

Lawrence J. Greene
Leigh Jones-Bamman

Introduction

Does This Sound Familiar?

John threw his backpack onto the bed and slammed the door to his room. He began pacing around the room. He had studied three hours for the history exam, and he had received only a **C−**. In frustration he kicked over the wastepaper basket.

"Why should I break my back studying for a test if the best I can do is **C−**?" he thought. "Even if I study, it doesn't seem to help at all."

That evening the atmosphere at the dinner table was terrible. John ended up getting into a big argument with his kid brother, and his dad asked both of them to leave the table.

Felicia also had studied very hard for the exam. As usual, she received a **B**. Although a **B** is a very decent grade, Felicia wanted to be an **A** student. Her goal was to become a psychologist, and she knew that she would need good grades to get into a good university. Despite all of her effort, she could not figure out what she needed to do to become an **A** student.

Susan took the same history exam. She would have been delighted to receive a **B** or even the **C−** that John received. But Susan received a **D**. "Well, I could have gotten an **F**," she thought as she walked home with her boyfriend. "Considering that I hardly studied at all, a **D** isn't so bad. Anyway, who cares? Steve and I are going to the movies on Friday evening, and summer vacation is only four weeks away."

It is easy to understand why John is so upset and frustrated. Despite all of his effort, a **C−** seems to be the best he can do.

Felicia is also frustrated. She senses that she can be a better student, but she doesn't know how to do **A** quality work.

No book can make Susan into a smarter student. Before Susan can do better in school, she will have to decide whether she wants to do better in school.

If you feel that your problems in school are similar to the problems that John, Felicia, or Susan are experiencing, you have four basic options:

1. You can give up and stop trying. or caring.
2. You can continue working hard in the hope that your grades will improve somehow.
3. You can continue working hard and accept the "fact" that you are not a good student and never will be.
4. You can learn new skills that will enable you to study more effectively and thus get better grades.

If you don't want to stop trying and you want to get the most from your effort, option 4 is your best choice. This book was written to help you achieve the goals in that option.

> Remember:
>
> There are no magic carpet rides to better grades.
> Learning how to study effectively takes time.
> Learning how to study effectively takes work.

PART I
Organizing Yourself

CHAPTER 1
Taking a Look at Yourself

Time Required: Approximately 35 Minutes

In this chapter you will examine
1. your present study habits
2. your priorities
3. your goals

Evaluating Your Study Habits

Understanding how you study is an important step in the process of improving your study habits. In this book the word *study* includes doing homework and preparing for tests.

The following checklist will help you see where you need improvement. Be honest with yourself. Fill out the checklist to reflect the way you are, not the way you think you should be.

Study Habits Checklist

Yes or No

1. Do you have goals for yourself? _____

2. If you have goals, are you working toward achieving them? _____

3. Do you usually have all the supplies you need to do your work at school? _____

4. Do you usually have all the supplies you need to do your work at home? _____

5. Do you usually write down your assignments? _____

6. Do you usually remember instructions? _____

7. Do you usually study in a quiet place? _____

8. Do you usually study without a lot of interruptions? _____

9. Do you have a written weekly schedule? _____

Look over your answers on the checklist. If you have answered *No* to any of the questions, the study skills in this book can help you. Learning them will make doing homework and studying for tests much easier.

Once you have completed the exercises in this book, you should be able to answer *Yes* to most, and perhaps all, of the same questions!

Establishing Priorities

Imagine that you are on a large sailboat in the Caribbean Sea. Suddenly you hit a floating log which rips a hole in the bow. You estimate that you have fifteen minutes before the boat sinks. There is a small lifeboat on board. You must quickly load it with the supplies you need to survive. You realize that it may be weeks before you are rescued.

Here is a list of the things on the sailboat that you may choose from to supply the lifeboat:

- Flashlight
- Batteries
- First-aid kit
- Dry clothes
- School books
- Bottled water
- Canned food
- Perfume
- Fishing gear

- Portable grill
- Portable radio transmitter
- Suntan lotion
- Travelers' checks
- Paper napkins
- Cassette tape recorder
- Hair dryer
- Flares

Now list the items in *order of importance* to your survival at sea. The most important item will be first on your list.

1. _____
2. _____
3. _____
4. _____
5. _____
6. _____
7. _____
8. _____
9. _____

10. _____
11. _____
12. _____
13. _____
14. _____
15. _____
16. _____
17. _____

Each person faced with the sinking boat situation will probably arrange the items on the list somewhat differently. Although you might decide that a first-aid kit is more important than a flashlight and batteries, it is clear that food and water should be placed at the top of the list. Food and water are essential to survival. Without them, it is doubtful that you could survive for more than two or three days.

The process of deciding what to take with you on the lifeboat involves **establishing priorities**. Establishing priorities means listing or ranking things in order of importance. The importance of some of the items will vary from person to person. For example, if you sunburn easily, taking suntan lotion is a priority. However, it should be apparent to *everyone* that flares and fishing gear are more important for survival than perfume or a hair dryer!

When you establish a priority, you decide that something is more important to you than something else. Establishing a priority is simply recognizing that something is meaningful or essential to you. Once you recognize a priority, the next step is to place that priority high on your list of things to do or accomplish.

Establishing goals for your life also involves establishing priorities. Suppose, for instance, that you want very much to become a fashion designer, but you are failing English. Your immediate priority is to figure out how to pass English. You recognize that if you don't pass the course, you will not graduate from high school. Very few employers will hire someone who hasn't graduated from high school.

A typical list of things to do follows. Pretend that you must arrange them in order of priority. Put the most important item first.

- Get a date for Friday night

- Clean up my room

- Change the strings on my guitar

- Study for the history midterm exam to be given tomorrow

- Buy tickets to next Sunday's concert

- Explain to the coach why I missed practice yesterday

- Go shopping for jeans

- Complete the chemistry problems that are due tomorrow

- Talk to my parents about increasing my allowance

- Recopy my English essay that is due by fourth period today

1. _____   6. _____

2. _____   7. _____

3. _____   8. _____

4. _____   9. _____

5. _____   10. _____

Although priorities will vary among people, most students will agree that the English essay, the chemistry problems, the history exam, and the discussion with the coach are very high priorities. The exact order of these priorities would depend on factors like the following:

- How long the English essay is and whether you have a study hall before fourth period

- How much studying remains to be done for the history test

- How long the chemistry problems should take to complete

- How upset the coach gets when you miss practice

At any given time, some activities are more important than others. Once you get in the habit of establishing priorities, you can use this skill to set goals for yourself.

Getting What You Want

When Jodi was in fifth grade and went to her first high school football game, she knew that she wanted to be a cheerleader someday. Being a cheerleader seemed exciting and glamorous to Jodi.

By the time Jodi entered high school, she was aware that there were girls in her class who were more coordinated and, perhaps, more popular than she was. Most of them also wanted to become cheerleaders. This did not discourage Jodi. She was certain that she would become a cheerleader.

To make the squad, Jodi realized that she would have to work very hard. She would have to be able to do each cheer better than anyone else trying out. She knew that she would have to project her enthusiasm, her personality, and her spirit.

Jodi also realized that she had to make sacrifices. Instead of spending her free time with her friends after school, Jodi worked for at least an hour practicing the cheers and the routines. After mastering one cheer, she would begin preparing and practicing the next one.

Jodi's practice and preparation paid off. She was selected to be on the freshman cheerleading squad and, later, she became the captain of the varsity squad.

You, too, can get what you want. Like Jodi, you must first establish goals and then work to achieve them. Jodi's long-term goal was to be a cheerleader, and her short-term goals were to master the cheers. You will find that short-term goals are necessary in order to achieve long-term goals.

Establishing Goals

When you define your goals, you provide yourself with a very important sense of direction. You become sure about where you are heading and what you need to achieve in order to get what you want out of life.

If you were to talk with the best students in your class about school, you would find that the majority of them have thought about their short-term and long-term goals. Typically, the best students define good grades as one of their most important short-term goals. Being accepted into college or getting a particular job is often one of their long-term goals.

Let's assume that you know what you want to do when you finish school: you have decided to become a veterinarian. To become a veterinarian, you probably know that first you must graduate from high school with good grades. After high school you must go to college and get good grades there. Finally, you must be accepted at a school of veterinary medicine. Because so many students want to become veterinarians, getting into such a school is extremely difficult. The programs are highly competitive, and only the best students are accepted.

Once you realize that becoming a veterinarian is not an easy process, you are faced with the challenge of figuring out how to achieve your goal. Here's the challenge:

Long-Term Goal: To become a veterinarian

Short-Term Goals (These goals may be monthly or yearly, but they must be achieved in order to reach the long-term goal.):

1. Take the required science courses.

2. Get good grades throughout four years of high school.

3. Impress your teachers with your performance so that they will recommend you for college.

4. Begin saving money for college expenses.

If you don't have any long-term goals, don't be discouraged. This is perfectly normal for a young person. Begin by getting used to thinking about your future. Once you do set some long-term goals for yourself, don't be afraid to change them. It is normal to change goals as you mature.

On page 12 you will find a sample **Goal Organizer**. It has been filled out to show you how a typical student might establish his or her goals. On page 13 you will find your own Goal Organizer. After you understand how the sample Goal Organizer has been filled out, complete your own Goal Organizer.

If you do have long-term goals, fill them in. If not, focus on short-term goals such as getting a good grade in your science class. Remember that *a good high school record will permit you to choose what you want to do with your life.*

Please note that weekly and daily goals have also been filled in on the sample Goal Organizer. Students who choose to establish daily and weekly goals for themselves will become "super organized." They probably will find that they have more free time than they realized!

Sample Goal Organizer

LONG-TERM GOALS

1. Graduate from high school with a **B** average or better.
2. Become a starter on the varsity basketball team.
3. Qualify for a college scholarship.
4. Become a lawyer.

SHORT-TERM GOALS

1. Receive a minimum of **B** on the next English book report.
2. Complete a review of the first six chapters in the history text.
3. Copy biology notes for the two days absent last week.
4. Receive a minimum of **B** on the next algebra test.

WEEKLY GOALS

1. Complete all science problems by Thursday.
2. Compare history notes with Joan.
3. Read a minimum of thirty pages in the novel for the next book report.
4. Review Spanish vocabulary from previous weeks.

DAILY GOALS

1. Check to make sure I have written down all assignments.
2. Be sure to hand in daily Spanish sentences on time.
3. Check to make sure I have all science handouts.
4. Get to gym class on time!

Goal Organizer

——————————— LONG-TERM GOALS ———————————

1.

2.

3.

4.

——————————— SHORT-TERM GOALS ———————————

1.

2.

3.

4.

——————————— WEEKLY GOALS ———————————

1.

2.

3.

4.

——————————— DAILY GOALS ———————————

1.

2.

3.

4.

Keeping Track of Your Achievements

Check off each goal as it is achieved. It's a good idea to replace each achievement with a new goal. Sometimes, however, you may simply want to achieve all of your goals, check them off, and then take it easy or "coast" for a while. You will have to decide if coasting is appropriate for you.

Achieving goals is something like losing weight. At first, people might not realize that you are getting thinner. As you continue to lose weight, however, your friends will start to become aware of the new you.

Each time you achieve your goals, give yourself a pat on the back. *You deserve to be acknowledged!* When you first start using this new system of establishing goals, your teachers and your parents may not recognize the improvement. They may not notice that your work is now handed in on time or that your assignment book is always organized. Results take time, but just remember: everyone will become aware of the new you as soon as they see your better grades.

Making Your Goals a Part of Your Life

It is a good idea to tape your Goal Organizer to the wall near your desk so that you can see it when you study. For fun, put your long-term goals in a sealed envelope. Put the envelope away. Every six months open the envelope and take a look at what you wrote. Change the goals if you wish, and reseal the envelope.

Establishing and reviewing goals can help make the sacrifices involved in getting an **A** on the chemistry exam seem worthwhile. Deciding to study while other kids are outside socializing can be a real test of how serious you are about achieving your goals. When you are certain of what your priorities are, having to discipline yourself becomes much less of a problem.

It is possible that your long-term goals will not change during your years in junior high school, high school, and college. But it is also possible that these long-term goals will undergo many changes as you get older. Don't be ashamed or afraid to change your mind about what you want to do with your life. A fifteen-year-old who wants to be a computer programmer or a basketball player has as much right to change career goals as a child who decides at four years of age that she wants to be a cowgirl when she grows up.

What You Have Learned in This Chapter:

1. *How to evaluate your study habits*

2. *How to establish priorities*

3. *How to establish short-term goals*

4. *How to establish long-term goals*

5. *How to keep track of your achievements*

CHAPTER 2
Getting Organized

Time Required: Approximately 35 Minutes

START HIGHLIGHTING

In this chapter you will learn

1. how to organize the materials you need for studying

2. how to organize your assignments

3. how to organize your notebook

4. how to remember information

Tools of the Trade

Roberto walked into class just as the bell rang. Almost immediately he began searching through his backpack for a pencil. The pack was crammed with loose papers, books, a pair of gym socks, the remains of his lunch, and other items that had been in the pack since the start of the school year.

The teacher began to go over some material that had been presented the previous day. It was material that Roberto hadn't understood. When Roberto realized that he had nothing to write with, he began to panic. In desperation he asked Tony for a pencil. Although Tony found one for him, Tony was clearly annoyed. It was the third time in a week that Roberto had asked to borrow a pencil, and he hadn't bothered to return the first two.

By the time Roberto was ready to start taking notes, the teacher had moved on to another topic.

Does this sound at all like you? If you have answered *Yes* to this question, you need to get organized!

How Do You Get Organized?

Imagine taking apart an airplane engine and just dropping the parts on the floor. After about five minutes, you discover that you do not have the proper wrenches to remove certain parts. Oil and grease are all over, and you do not have any rags to clean the parts off. Despite these problems, you finally manage to disassemble the engine. You somehow figure out that a certain part is defective, and you realize that you will have to order a new one. But you don't know what the part is called, and you can't find the manual which lists and identifies the parts. It also dawns on you that without the manual, you will never be able to put the engine back together again!

Perhaps you are thinking that you would never be stupid enough to take apart an engine without the necessary tools and without an instruction manual.

But do you sometimes begin a homework assignment or study for a test without having the necessary books or supplies to do the job correctly?

Organization is the key—not only to taking an engine apart but also to doing well in school. The first step in getting organized is making sure you have all the things you need to do the job.

Here is a checklist of most of the materials you will need to do your homework and your studying. Please note that extra space is provided for you to add those special things you will need for certain classes.

Two detachable copies of the **Supply Checklist** have been provided at the end of the book. Tape one to the inside of your notebook. Leave the other copy at home on the desk where you study.

Don't forget to take everything on your Supply Checklist with you when you leave for school in the morning!

Supply Checklist

———— MATERIALS NEEDED AT HOME ————

Paper	_____	Assignment Sheet	_____
Pens	_____	Hole Punch	_____
Pencils	_____	Watch or Clock	_____
Binder	_____	School Books	_____
Ruler	_____	Phone Number of One Student in Each Class	_____
Class Schedule	_____	_____	_____
Calculator	_____	_____	_____
Dictionary	_____	_____	_____
Pencil Sharpener	_____	_____	_____

```
┌─────────────────────────────────────────────────────────────┐
│ ───────── MATERIALS NEEDED AT SCHOOL ─────────               │
│                                                              │
│   Paper          _____    Assignment Sheet    _____        │
│                                                              │
│   Pens           _____    Hole Punch          _____        │
│                                                              │
│   Pencils        _____    Watch or Clock      _____        │
│                                                              │
│   Binder         _____    Completed Homework  _____        │
│                                                              │
│   Class Schedule _____    Gym Clothes         _____        │
│                                                              │
│   Calculator     _____    _____    _____        │
│                                                              │
│   Dictionary     _____    _____                  │
│                                                              │
│   School Books   _____    _____    _____        │
│                                                              │
└─────────────────────────────────────────────────────────────┘
```

Why Do I Need a Checklist?

It's 6:15 A.M. Someone is already in the operating room of the hospital—ahead of both the surgeon and the patient. That person is the scrub nurse, and he is preparing and arranging the instruments that the surgeon might need for the operation.

The instruments are placed in a certain order on the nurse's tray. Using a checklist, the scrub nurse organizes the scalpels, the scissors, the clamps, the retractors, the thread, the sponges, the needles, and the bandages. If the nurse did not go through this routine with the checklist, there's a good chance that he would forget something essential.

Once the nurse has followed this procedure many times, a written checklist may no longer be necessary. A mental checklist may be sufficient. But until the nurse reaches that point, he will need to check things off on a written list. With practice, getting organized becomes second nature.

You, too, will probably need a written checklist in the beginning. Once you master the routine of organizing yourself, a written checklist may no longer be required. With practice, you may be able to remember all of the materials you will need to do your homework or study for a test. But until you do master the routine, it's best to get in the habit of checking off the things you need *before* you start.

Keeping Track

People with photographic memories may not have to write things down. But unless you have a photographic memory, you are going to need a notebook or an assignment book. Very few students can remember everything about an assignment without writing it down.

There are different ways to keep track. The one we suggest is an **Assignment Sheet**. The Assignment Sheet not only will permit you to check off each assignment as it is completed, but it also will alert you to when the next test or report is due.

As you fill in your Assignment Sheet each week, it is important to include **page numbers, unit sections, problem numbers,** and any special **instructions, tips, or comments** from your teacher. These can be very valuable aids that will help you to complete your assignments with less difficulty. For example, if your English teacher assigns an essay on a certain topic, he or she may require

- that the essay be written in ink
- that it be no more than one page long
- that it be legible

Unless you have written down and have carefully followed these special instructions, you may find yourself getting no credit for the essay.

Below you will find two ways to fill in an Assignment Sheet. The same assignments have been reported in both examples. The first example is complete. The second example is not complete. A great deal of important information about the assignments has been left out. Without this information, the homework may be done incorrectly.

Correct Way to Fill In Assignment Sheet

Subjects	English	Math	French	Drafting	Speech	History
Monday Oct. 7	Creative Story due Thursday. Description of a pencil at least two paragraphs. rough draft.	pg. 457 # 1-15 odds only show all work	Study for test, know vocab., verb tenses and translation Test on Wednesday	Work on project from chapter 3 due on Friday	Work on speech due Friday — must be humorous — under four minutes.	Answer questions on pg. 309 # 1-7 complete sentences Look back in text.
Date of Next Test	Oct. 14		Oct. 9			
Next Report Due						Nov. 5

Incorrect Way to Fill In Assignment Sheet

Subjects	English	Math	French	Drafting	Speech	History
Monday Oct. 7	Description of a pencil- due Thurs.	do problems on pg. 457	test on Wednesday	project	speech due Friday	pg. 309
Date of Next Test	Oct. 14		Oct. 9			
Next Report Due						Nov. 5

Here is a sample Assignment Sheet that has been completed for an entire week. Please note that the dates when tests are scheduled and reports are due have been filled in. If you have any questions about how to fill in your own Assignment Sheet, refer to this sample.

You'll find your own Assignment Sheet at the back of the book. Make copies and use them for recording your weekly assignments. Put an Assignment Sheet in the front of your binder. Get into the habit of using it. Soon it will become second nature for you to write your assignments in a specific place. When you are finished with an assignment, check it off. But don't cross out the assignment! You may need to refer to it later.

After you become more organized, you may want to design your own Assignment Sheet.

Sample Assignment Sheet

Subjects	English	Math	French	Drafting	Speech	History
Monday Oct. 7	creative story due Thursday. Description of a pencil- at least two paragraphs- rough draft.	pg. 457 #1-15 odds only. show all work	Study for test know vocab., verb tenses + Translation - Test on Wed.	Work on project from Chapter 3- due on friday	Work on speech due Friday- must be humorous - under 4 min.	Answer quest. pg. 309 #1-7 complete sentences. Look back in text.
Tuesday Oct. 8	creative story- (see mon.)	handout due on Tues.	Study for test (see Mon.)	project (see Mon.)	speech (see Mon.)	Read chapter 4- pgs. 313- 333
Wednesday Oct. 9	creative story (see Mon.)	handout due on Tues.		project (see Mon.)	speech (see Mon.)	Read Chapter 4 pgs 334- 354
Thursday Oct 10.			pg. 45 exercises A, B + D	project (see Mon.)	speech (see Mon.)	
Friday Oct. 11	study for test		Read and translate pgs. 46-47			Outline for report due Monday. see handout
Date of Next Test	Oct. 14		Oct. 9			
Next Report Due						Nov. 5

Organizing Your Notebook

1. Keep a copy of your schedule in the front of your notebook.

2. Attach a plastic pouch to your notebook to hold pens, pencils, a ruler, a hole punch, and any other materials you might need.

3. Punch holes in all assignments and work sheets that are passed out by the teacher, and insert them in your notebook.

4. Divide your notebook into sections—one section for each subject.

5. Put dates on your notes. It will be much easier for you to find specific information when your notes are dated. With this system, you can tell which days' notes you missed by being absent from school.

6. Keep extra paper at the back of your notebook.

Improving Your Memory

Every day there are hundreds of things that you need to remember: locking your locker, brushing your hair, keeping an appointment after school. Some of the daily tasks have become habits because you have been doing them for a long time. You don't have to think about them. You automatically brush your teeth, get dressed, and have breakfast in the morning. Imagine if you forgot the routine and showed up for your first class with your bathrobe on!

Not everything that you have to remember is a habit. When your parents ask you to write to your grandmother or when you have to buy some tickets after school, you must make a conscious effort to remember these things. Unless you make a conscious effort to remember, you might forget.

Seven Methods to Help You Remember

The first group of steps will remind you that *you have something to remember*.

1. **Review in your mind what you will need to take with you or do whenever you are going somewhere.**

   Stop before you walk out the door and ask yourself, "Do I have everything I need? What are the things I have to do today?" Keys, homework, money, and school books are all easy to forget. *Making a conscious effort to think about your responsibilities and to organize them in your mind develops good memory habits.*

2. **Wear your watch or rings in an unfamiliar way.**

   If you always wear your watch or rings in a certain way, you become used to having them that way. If you switch your watch to the other wrist or wear a ring on a different finger, it will feel funny. The strange feeling will remind you that you have to remember something. Just don't forget what it is you are trying to remember!

3. **Ask someone to remind you.**

   This method will work only if the person you ask to remind you is reliable.

The second group of steps will help you to remember *specific information*.

4. Write it down.

This is the best way to remember, especially if you have a long list of things to do, or if you have something *very* important to remember. Just make sure you don't lose the paper you've written it on!

5. Say it to yourself, repeating each item at least five times.

Repeating a list out loud is even better than saying it to yourself. This technique is especially helpful for memorizing spelling or vocabulary words, history facts, and other types of information you may need to know for a quiz or an exam. *Repeating things makes information stick in your memory.*

6. Create a picture in your mind of what you're trying to remember.

Later, when you need to remember, you can pull the picture from your mind. With this technique you can picture yourself doing something or picture the way something looks (such as a map of the United States). Details will be easier to remember this way. *Visualization helps you to store what you're trying to remember.*

7. Make up a formula or sentence.

Music students, for example, who are trying to remember the lines and spaces on the treble clef (E, G, B, D, F) will often use each of those letters to make a sentence: **E**very **G**ood **B**oy **D**oes **F**ine. The sentence is easier to remember than the letters alone. *Putting information into a sentence or formula can make remembering difficult information easier.*

You will not use all these techniques at once. Different situations call for different methods, and you may find that one method works better than another for you. On the next page, you will practice these memory techniques.

Practicing Your New Memory Techniques

Below are some situations which involve memory. In each situation, a different technique should be used. Match the situation to the technique which best fits the situation. Place the letter of the technique you have chosen in the space provided. Use each technique only once.

Memory Techniques

A. Review in your mind what you will need to take with you or do before you go anywhere.

B. Wear your watch or rings in an unfamiliar way.

C. Ask someone to remind you.

D. Write it down.

E. Say it to yourself.

F. Visualize.

G. Make up a formula or sentence.

Situations

1. _____ You see a notice on a bulletin board for a free golden retriever puppy. You've always wanted one, but you never could afford the high price. You run to a phone booth to call and get directions to the house. You discover that you do not have anything to write on. How do you remember the directions?

2. _____ You have a part in the school play. You have to memorize your lines. How do you remember?

3. _____ You are going to the grocery store to buy food for the club's weekend trip. How do you remember the necessary supplies?

4. _____ You and your sister are leaving the house for a day of hiking. Your mother reminds you both that you must take your allergy pills in two hours. How do you remember to take your pills?

5. _____ School is over for the day. You're in a hurry to get home. You have several important homework assignments due tomorrow. How do you remember to bring home all the books you need to do your assignments?

6. _____ You are riding your bike down the street. You see a car back out of a parking space, hit a car that is parked behind it, and leave a large dent in the parked car's fender. The driver of the car leaves the scene of the accident without leaving a note. You have seen the car's license plate, but you do not have a pencil and paper. How do you remember the license plate number?

7. _____ You are in the garage, building some shelves for your room. Your father comes in to tell you that a friend has telephoned and wants you to call back. You know that you won't be finished with your project for at least an hour. How do you remember to return the call?

Answers

(Remember, your answers may be different. You can use more than one technique in many of the situations.)

1. __F__ As the person on the phone gives you directions, try to picture the streets (if you know them). Visualize the route you will be traveling. Also, try to think of landmarks you know.

2. __E__ Say the lines aloud, over and over. It's the repetition that helps you to memorize those lines.

3. __D__ Making a list and writing it down is the best way to remember a lot of information.

4. __C__ If your sister is reliable, the two of you can help each other to remember.

5. __A__ Take the time to think about what you need to take with you *before* you leave school. It takes only a minute, and this extra time and effort may save you a lot of pain later on.

6. __G__ Make up a sentence that has meaning using the numbers and letters from the license plate. For example, if the plate is B 75 RFM, you could say: But 75 roses for me!

7. __B__ When you're in the middle of a project, you may not be able to write something down. Switching your watch or rings is an easy thing to do.

Stop right now and think about which techniques you use for remembering things. If you don't use all of these techniques, you may want to try them the next time you have to remember something.

Getting Organized

THE COACH SUGGESTS AN EXPERIMENT

Geoff was one of the better swimmers on the varsity squad. His ambition was to win a swimming scholarship to a university with a nationally ranked team. To get the scholarship, Geoff knew that he needed to improve his time in the breast stroke. The coach agreed that Geoff had the potential to become a better swimmer, but he would have to change some bad habits. The coach told Geoff that he needed to work on his dive and his turns. He suggested an experiment. Geoff would record his best time at practice. He would then spend one extra hour each day after practice learning some new techniques. At the end of the week he would compare his time in the hundred meter breast stroke with his time before he began the experiment. This would prove whether or not the new techniques were working.

You are now going to do your own experiment in improving your organizational skills.

Experiment 1

Part A: Evaluating Your Organizational Skills

How well organized do you think you are? Take the time to honestly evaluate your current organizational skills, using the checklist below.

Code

0 = Poor   **1** = Fair   **2** = Good   **3** = Excellent

1. I always have the materials I need to study at home. _____

2. I always have the materials I need to do my work in school. _____

3. I always write down my assignments. _____

Total Score _____

If you have given yourself a total score of 9, you do *not* need to do the rest of this experiment. If your score is less than 9, do Parts B and C.

Part B: Completing the Checklist

Each day during the next week complete the following checklist. Place a **Y** (yes) or an **N** (no) for each day of the week. Give yourself a **Y** only if you used the Supply Checklist (pages 16 and 17) and the Assignment Sheet (page 123) as you were taught in this chapter.

Y = Yes, I used the list properly.

N = No, I did not use the list properly.

	Mon.	Tues.	Wed.	Thurs.	Fri.	Sat.	Sun.
Date:	_____	_____	_____	_____	_____	_____	_____
Used Supply Checklist							
Used Assignment Sheet							

Part C: Reevaluating Your Organizational Skills

Now that you have kept track of the ways in which you organize yourself for studying, rate your organizational skills in the same way you did in Part A of this experiment.

Code

0 = Poor   **1** = Fair   **2** = Good   **3** = Excellent

1. I always have the materials I need to study.   _____

2. I always have the materials I need to do my work
   in school.   _____

3. I always write down my assignments.   _____

Total Score   _____

Compare your present score with your original one on page 24. Your total score should be much higher! If it is not, redo the experiment for another week. Make a special effort to use the Supply Checklist and the Assignment Sheet.

Now that your organizational skills have improved, it is important that you continue using the Supply Checklist and the Assignment Sheet so that the new organizational skills you have learned will become part of your daily routine.

What You Have Learned in This Chapter:

1. *How to organize the materials you need for studying*

2. *How to organize your assignments*

3. *How to organize your notebook*

4. *How to remember information*

CHAPTER 3
Getting Ready to Study

Time Required: Approximately 35 Minutes

In this chapter you will learn

1. how to evaluate your study environment

2. how to improve the quality of your studying

Choosing the Right Environment

Imagine a surgeon doing an operation in the middle of the hospital cafeteria. As she is about to make the incision, someone yells for a cheeseburger with onions. Above the noise, the surgeon tries to tell her assistant that she needs a special instrument. Distracted by the noise and commotion in the room, the assistant hands her the wrong instrument. The surgeon is also distracted and discovers that she has been given the wrong instrument only after she has already attached it to the patient.

Of course, this little nightmare would never happen. A surgeon would operate only under the best of conditions. The room would be quiet so that she could concentrate. She would be well rested. The other staff in the operating room would be well trained. All of the instruments and equipment that the surgeon might need would be on hand and in good operating condition.

Checking Out Your Environment

Below you will find some situations which you might encounter during the course of a typical week. Match each situation with the environment you feel is appropriate.

_____ 1. Flirting

_____ 2. Studying for the history midterm

_____ 3. Playing volleyball

_____ 4. Doing chemistry problems

_____ 5. Recopying biology notes

_____ 6. Talking about the cute boy or girl you just met

_____ 7. Sanding and varnishing your new desk

_____ 8. Studying your lines for the school play

_____ 9. Writing a report on Egypt

_____ 10. Reading the newspaper

_____ 11. Organizing the art work for the school car wash fund raiser

A. In the library

B. On the school lawn

C. Sitting at your desk

D. On the telephone

E. While listening to the stereo

F. In study hall

G. In the shop in the garage

H. Sitting on the floor

I. In the gym

J. Sitting in a comfortable chair in your room

K. At the kitchen table

Answers

1. B	7. G
2. C	8. J
3. I	9. A
4. F	10. E
5. K	11. H
6. D	

Some of your answers may differ from those above. For example, you could choose to study for the history midterm in the library, in study hall, or sitting at your desk. It would not be a good idea, however, to study for the midterm while listening to the stereo. If there's no one to disturb you in the kitchen, the kitchen table might be an excellent place to study. But if other members of the family are working there or are walking in and out, you will have a difficult time concentrating. Why make studying harder for yourself? *Choose the place where you can do your best work!*

A Quiet Place to Work

How do you feel when you're at a movie and the people behind you are talking? Most likely, you feel irritated because you can't concentrate on the movie.

Have you ever tried to talk to your friend on the phone and listen to your mother at the same time? Listening to two conversations can be tough. Your mom may be telling you to turn on the oven at 5:00 at the same time that your friend is telling you how Andrea and Lamar just broke up. You may miss out on important parts of both conversations.

Most people's brains can't pay attention to two things at once. When someone talks at a movie, your brain has to put out a great deal of effort to block out the noise. When you try to listen to two conversations, your brain concentrates on one conversation for a second. Then it switches to the other. Your concentration jumps back and forth. You are unable to get the full story from either person.

When you do your homework, your brain needs to focus only on what you are doing. If you listen to music or watch TV while studying, your brain can't work properly. Part of your attention will be directed toward your homework. Part of your attention will be directed toward the music or TV. Why cheat yourself? Turn off the stereo or TV while you are studying. Your brain will focus completely on your homework. You'll make fewer mistakes, and you'll get done sooner. Then you can watch TV or listen to music and enjoy it.

What's the Best Position for Studying?

There has always been a certain amount of controversy about whether it is better for students to study sitting at a desk, in an easy chair, lying on a bed, or lying on the floor. Although there are many teachers and parents who would argue that proper studying can take place only when the student is sitting in a chair at a desk, what's truly important is whether or not you feel mentally alert when you are studying.

When you study, you will know if you are using your study time effectively. If you find that you are spending a lot of time changing positions, daydreaming, or becoming sleepy when you are sitting in a comfortable chair or lying on your bed, then clearly you need to consider studying in a different position. Try sitting at a desk or at a table, and see if that helps you remain alert.

Although there are exceptions, most good students choose to sit at a desk when they study. They do so because sitting at a desk helps them to concentrate, to remain alert, and to make the most effective use of their time.

Study Breaks

You've been looking at the same page for ten minutes, and you still can't understand what the author is saying. It's not surprising. It's 10:45 at night, and you've been studying for four hours straight.

It's time for a break. Your mind can function efficiently only for so long, and then it starts to slow down. By taking a break and perhaps drinking a glass of milk and munching on a snack, you are giving your brain a well-deserved rest.

Sometimes too many breaks can get in the way of learning. They can be used as an escape from the hard work involved in preparing a report or studying for an exam.

Good students know how and when to schedule their breaks. The purpose of a break is to reduce fatigue and to permit you to recharge your mental battery. *Study breaks are necessary. But they should not be used as an excuse for not studying.*

A good study break formula for students in sixth through ninth grades is:

$$30 \text{ minutes of work } + \text{ a 10-minute break}$$

A good study break formula for high school students is:

$$45 \text{ minutes of work } + \text{ a 10-minute break}$$

If you find yourself working for periods which are too long and exhaust you, consider shortening your study time. If you find yourself getting up from your desk every five or ten minutes, gradually increase the duration of your work periods.

An alarm clock or a timer can help you regulate your study periods. When the time is up, give yourself a ten-minute break. Get up and walk around. Have a snack. Get your blood flowing again.

When your ten-minute break is up, get back to work for another half hour. For some students, getting back to studying after the ten-minute break is very difficult. The prospect of working is frequently less appealing than the prospect of staying in the kitchen and having another glass of milk and another apple. Setting the timer or alarm clock even during your breaks may be necessary until you develop greater willpower.

Increasing your work time so that you can study for an hour at a stretch will require a lot of discipline. Once you increase your work time to an hour, you might decide to reward yourself with a fifteen-minute break instead of a ten-minute break.

Studying for more than three hours during an evening is seldom productive for students in junior high school. Four hours of studying should be the maximum for high school students. If you study for longer periods, your mind won't work as efficiently, and it may take you twice as long to learn something as it would if you were feeling fresh.

Interruptions

They all were nervous as they set up their equipment in the studio. This was the band's first record. It had taken three years of hard work to get this break. Finally, everything was ready, and they could start the recording session.

The studio was in the downtown area of the city, and the only parking place near the studio that the band could find was in a thirty-minute tow-away zone. If they didn't put a quarter in the meter every thirty minutes, their van would be towed away.

Every half hour, someone had to run out of the studio and deposit a quarter in the meter. The other members of the band had to stop playing and wait for the person to return. Needless to say, the recording session was a disaster.

It is impossible to do your best work when you are constantly being interrupted. Sometimes interruptions are caused by other people such as a little brother or sister who has a habit of coming into your room to ask questions. In other cases you are responsible for the interruptions. You may start fiddling with something on your desk. Or you may decide five minutes after you have begun studying that you simply must call your best friend to find out what is happening on Friday night.

You may need the help of your entire family to reduce the number of interruptions when you are studying. Explain to them that you will be working for thirty or forty-five minutes at a time and that you don't want to be interrupted during that time. If someone telephones you, ask your family to take a message. Then during your ten-minute break you can call back your friend, have a snack, or talk with your family.

It is difficult to force yourself to do something that you are not particularly interested in doing. If you don't enjoy biology, studying for a biology exam can require a lot of discipline. Although studying for a subject that doesn't interest you can be unpleasant, the fact is that if you don't study, your grades will suffer. If you are going to study, you might as well do a good job of it. This means studying efficiently and without frequent interruptions.

It's interesting how important and urgent certain things become when you are in your room studying. The plants may indeed need watering, the dog may indeed need to be brushed, and the record that is on the stereo may indeed be wonderful to listen to, but these things can all wait until your break time. These things are much less urgent when you have plenty of free time to do them.

If you are able to study without interruptions, you will find that you will get your work done faster, and you will do a better job. This will leave you more time to do the things you want to do.

Experiment 2

Part A: Evaluating Your Study Habits

How good are your study habits? Take the time to honestly evaluate your current studying style, using the following checklist.

Code

0 = Poor   **1** = Fair   **2** = Good   **3** = Excellent

1. I study sitting at a desk or table.   _____

2. I study in a quiet environment.   _____

3. I study for thirty to forty-five minutes before taking a break.   _____

4. I take only a ten- to fifteen-minute break.   _____

5. I study without frequent interruptions.   _____

Total Score   _____

If you have given yourself a score of 15, you do *not* need to finish this experiment. If your score is less than 15, do Parts B and C.

Part B: Completing the Checklist

During the next seven days use the techniques you have learned in this chapter when you study. At the end of each day, complete the checklist and evaluate yourself. Give yourself a **Y** (yes) for each study habit you did use and an **N** (no) for each study habit you did not use.

Y = Yes   **N** = No

	Mon.	Tues.	Wed.	Thurs.	Fri.	Sat.	Sun.
Studied Sitting at a Desk							
Quiet Environment (No TV or Music)							
Studied for Thirty to Forty-five Minutes Without a Break							
Took Only Ten- to Fifteen-Minute Breaks							
No Interruptions During Study Time							

Part C: Reevaluating Your Study Habits

Now that you have kept track of your new study habits for a week, rate your study effectiveness in the same way you did in Part A of this experiment.

Code

0 = Poor   **1** = Fair   **2** = Good   **3** = Excellent

1. I study sitting at a desk or table.   _____

2. I study in a quiet environment.   _____

3. I study for thirty to forty-five minutes before
    taking a break.   _____

4. I take only a ten- to fifteen-minute break.   _____

5. I study without frequent interruptions.   _____

Total Score   _____

Compare your present score with your original one.

Your total score should now be much higher! If it is not, try the experiment for another week. Make a special effort to use the study effectiveness techniques in the experiment.

What You Have Learned in This Chapter:

1. *How to choose the best study environments*

2. *Why you need to study in a quiet place*

3. *How to choose the best position for studying*

4. *How to schedule study breaks*

5. *How to resist distractions and interruptions*

CHAPTER 4
Scheduling Your Time

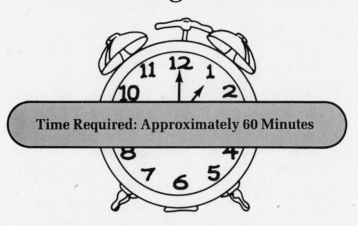

Time Required: Approximately 60 Minutes

In this chapter you will learn

1. how to design your personal weekly schedule

2. how to plan the use of your study time

What's a Schedule For?

As the plane approaches the San Francisco airport, you can hardly wait. One whole week in Northern California! You mentally run through all of the things you want to see: the cable cars, Fisherman's Wharf, the Golden Gate Bridge, the ferry boat to Sausalito, Chinatown, Big Sur, boutiques, the planetarium, the zoo, the beach . . .

Your family has agreed to spend two or three days in San Francisco and do some local sightseeing. After seeing San Francisco, the family will rent a car, drive down the coast, and spend three days camping in Big Sur.

As you think about all of the things you want to do, you wonder whether you and your family will have the time for everything. As usual, your mom has set up an itinerary and a schedule. Knowing how well organized she is, you're sure that she's planned for everything.

Some people shudder when they think about using a schedule. They think that by using a schedule they will lose their freedom. These people fear that they can no longer be spontaneous if they are committed to an inflexible schedule.

Schedules can restrict you. But they also can free you by making your time go further. Imagine how much extra time you will have to spend with your friends, watch TV, listen to music, or do other things that you enjoy if you can learn how to use your time efficiently.

A schedule helps you to balance your time. It permits you to decide how much time you need to do the things that must be done. Once you organize your time, you will be surprised at how much free time you can have.

Schedules are not chiseled in stone. They can be designed to be both flexible and tailored to your needs. If something unexpected comes up, such as a surprise quiz, it's all right to adjust your schedule. The purpose of the schedule is to provide you with a framework for using your time efficiently. Once you begin using your time more efficiently, you will find that you are achieving more *and* enjoying more free time than you did before!

How You Spend Your Time

For any schedule to be of value, it has to *work* for you. To make a schedule work, you must first decide

1. what things need to be done

2. how much time is available for doing them

Before you attempt to make a schedule for yourself, write down how you spend your time during the next week. On the next page, you will find a sample **Weekly Time Chart** that will show you how to keep track of your daily activities during a typical school week. The Time Chart on page 38 has been left blank so that you can fill in the information that describes your own typical week.

Once you understand how the sample Weekly Time Chart has been filled in, you will be ready to complete your own Weekly Time Chart. Write in the time you spend sleeping, eating, going to school, doing homework, watching TV, seeing friends, talking on the phone, and so on. Also include things that you do as the need arises, like cleaning your room, going to see the dentist, and buying gifts. Some activities could fit into more than one category. If that happens, place such activities in the category that you think is best. Be sure to write down exactly what you did, and not what you think you should have done!

In some cases, you may have to estimate the number of hours spent on a certain activity, such as "time with friends." Because you're estimating, your totals each day may not always add up to twenty-four hours.

Sample Weekly Time Chart

Actual Number of Hours Spent During the Week of ___Oct. 7___

	Monday	Tuesday	Wednesday	Thursday	Friday	Saturday	Sunday
Sleeping	8	8	7½	7	8	8½	8
Eating and dressing	1½	1½	1½	1½	2½	1½	2½
School*	6½	6½	6½	6½	7		
Homework	2½	3	1½	2½	1½	1	2
Job*						4	
Sports*	1½		1½	1½			
Time alone (reading, etc.)	1		1			1	3
Time with family		1		2			5
Time with friends			2		3	7	1
TV and radio	1	1		1			
Clubs		2½	½	½			2
Chores	½	½	½	½	½	½	½
Telephone	1		½	1	1		
Miscellaneous		½				1	½

*Include transportation time.

Here is your Weekly Time Chart. At the end of each day, fill in the approximate number of hours you spent on each activity.

Weekly Time Chart

Actual Number of Hours Spent During the Week of _____

	Monday	Tuesday	Wednesday	Thursday	Friday	Saturday	Sunday
Sleeping							
Eating and dressing							
School*							
Homework							
Job*							
Sports*							
Time alone (reading, etc.)							
Time with family							
Time with friends							
TV and radio							
Clubs							
Chores							
Telephone							
Miscellaneous							

*Include transportation time.

Six Steps to Designing Your Own Schedule

1. Look at the sample **Weekly Schedule** on page 40. This will show you how a typical student might fill out his or her schedule.

2. Use colored pens or pencils to fill in your own Weekly Schedule (on page 41) with the "Must Do" categories. These are activities that you have to do at a certain time each day or week. The activities include

   - sleeping
   - eating
   - dressing
   - going to school
   - going to work
   - doing chores

3. Decide how much time you should spend each day doing homework. Use your Weekly Time Chart as a guide. Let's say that you now spend an average of two hours a day doing your homework. Do you honestly feel that this is enough time for you to do your best work? Write down here how many hours a day you have decided to spend doing homework.

Homework/Study Time Each Day:_____

4. Decide when you want to do your homework each day. Some students study best in the early evening, and some students do their best studying in the morning. Don't schedule yourself to study from 9:00 P.M. to 10:30 P.M. if you are usually sleepy by then. Remember also to schedule your homework so that you study for thirty to forty-five minutes and then take time out for a ten-minute break.

5. Use colored pens and pencils to fill in your homework time on your Weekly Schedule.

6. Use colored pens and pencils to fill in the other scheduled activities on your Weekly Schedule. These include

   - club functions
   - sports
   - chores
   - activities with your family
   - any activities that are a regular part of your life

You may find that you do not have enough time in the day for all the things you want to do. If so, you may have to cut some activities out.

Now that you have scheduled your activities, the rest of your time is free for you to do with as you wish! You can goof off, watch TV, join another club, take a snooze outdoors under a tree—whatever! It's your time.

You probably will not be able to keep to your schedule all the time. Things that aren't planned come up. For example, your history teacher may decide to give a quiz on the following day, and you will have to find some extra time in your schedule to study.

Once you design a schedule that works for you, you may still need to revise it from time to time. As you become a smarter and more efficient student, you may find that you do not have to spend as much time studying for tests or doing your homework. This means more free time!

Sample Weekly Schedule

	Monday	Tuesday	Wednesday	Thursday	Friday	Saturday	Sunday
A.M. 12–6	Sleeping	Sleeping	Sleeping	Sleeping	Sleeping	Sleeping	Sleeping
6–7	Dressing	Dressing	Dressing	Dressing	Dressing	Dressing	Dressing
7–8	School	School	School	School	School	School	School
8–9	Eating	Eating	Eating	Eating	Eating	Eating	Eating
9–10	School	School	School	School	School	Working	
10–11	School	School	School	School	School	Working	
11–12	School	School	School	School	School	Working	
P.M. 12–1	Eating	Eating	Eating	Eating	Eating	Eating	Eating
1–2	School	School	School	School	School	Working	
2–3	School	School	School	School	School		
3–4	Sports		Sports		Sports		
4–5	Sports	Club	Sports	Club	Sports		Homework
5–6							Homework
6–7	Eating	Eating	Eating	Eating	Eating	Eating	Eating
7–8	Homework	Homework	Homework				Homework
8–9	Homework	Homework	Homework				
9–10							
10–11	Sleeping	Sleeping	Sleeping	Sleeping			Sleeping
11–12	Sleeping	Sleeping	Sleeping	Sleeping		Sleeping	Sleeping

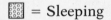

= Sleeping   = Playing sports

= Dressing and doing chores   = Doing homework

= Going to school   = Eating meals

= Working   = Going to club meetings

Your Weekly Schedule

	Monday	Tuesday	Wednesday	Thursday	Friday	Saturday	Sunday
A.M. 12–6							
6–7							
7–8							
8–9							
9–10							
10–11							
11–12							
P.M. 12–1							
1–2							
2–3							
3–4							
4–5							
5–6							
6–7							
7–8							
8–9							
9–10							
10–11							
11–12							

☐ = _____   ☐ = _____

☐ = _____   ☐ = _____

☐ = _____   ☐ = _____

☐ = _____   ☐ = _____

Remember:

1. Decide honestly how much time you need to spend on homework.

2. Make gradual adjustments in scheduling your study time.

3. Decide at what time of day you do your best studying.

4. Allow for "emergency" studying.

5. Make sure your schedule includes free time.

6. Design a schedule you can stick to for at least one week.

7. Revise your schedule when necessary.

What You Have Learned in This Chapter:

1. *How to plan the use of your study time*

2. *How to design your weekly schedule*

Review of Part I
Organizing Yourself

In Part I of this book you have learned how to

1. set your goals and priorities

2. organize your materials for studying

3. use an assignment sheet

4. remember information

5. choose the best study environments

6. set up a weekly schedule

How much of what you have learned have you actually put to use? The following checklist will help you identify the improvements you have made in your organizational skills.

Be honest with yourself. Fill out the checklist to reflect the way you are and not the way you think you should be.

Study Habits Checklist

Yes or No

1. Do you have goals for yourself? _____

2. If you have goals, are you working toward achieving them? _____

3. Do you usually have all the supplies you need to do your work at school? _____

4. Do you usually have all the supplies you need to do your work at home? _____

5. Do you usually write down your assignments? _____

6. Do you usually remember instructions? _____

7. Do you usually study in a quiet place? _____

8. Do you usually study without a lot of interruptions? _____

9. Do you have a written weekly schedule? _____

Do you recognize the Study Habits Checklist? You may recall that you completed the very same checklist when you began using this book. Look back now to the original checklist on page 7 and compare your current answers with your original ones. Have your study habits improved? If they haven't, pick one or two areas that you are willing to change and concentrate on improving those. Once you master these areas, you can begin working on one or two more.

PART II
Effective Studying

Evaluating Your Reading Habits

The following checklist will help you determine how well you understand and remember material that you read for school. Fill out the checklist to reflect the way you are and not the way you think you should be. If you feel the correct answer is *sometimes*, decide if the answer is more often *Yes* or more often *No*.

Reading Habits Checklist

	Yes or No
1. Do you think about what the material is covering *before* you begin to read?	_____
2. Do you think about what the material is covering *while* you are reading?	_____
3. Do you review in your mind what you have learned *after* you have read an assignment?	_____
4. Are you able to pick out the main ideas *while* you read?	_____
5. Can you decide what is important to remember?	_____
6. Do you know how to take notes on what you have read?	_____
7. Are you able to remember information about what you have read?	_____

If you have answered *No* to any of the questions above, the techniques in Part II can help you

1. to read material and better understand it

2. to remember what you have read

3. to take organized notes on what you have read

CHAPTER 5
The Active Thinking Method

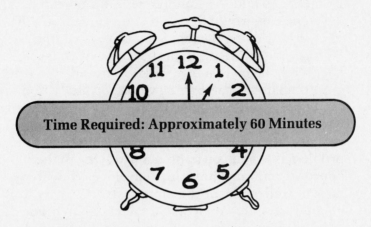

Time Required: Approximately 60 Minutes

In this chapter you will learn

1. how to understand what you have read

2. how to remember what you have read

Different Styles

The bell was about to ring at the end of science class, and Mr. Yee assigned Chapter 4 to be read for the next day. He told the students that the material in the chapter would be discussed during the remainder of the week, and a chapter test would be given on Friday.

Susan didn't bother to read the material. She figured she'd find out what the chapter was about when it was discussed in class.

That evening John read the material in Chapter 4. Although John seldom received good grades, he thought he was a very hard-working student. He felt that if he read the chapter, he would be prepared for the class discussion.

Felicia also read the chapter. She decided to try a reading method called the Active Thinking Method, which her sister had shown her. Her sister was a student in college and always received good grades. The method required more study time, but Felicia knew that it worked for her sister.

The next day in class, the teacher began the discussion by asking John how industrial pollution could affect the food chain in rivers. John vaguely recalled having read something in Chapter 4 about food chains and industrial pollution, but he hadn't thought about the relationship between the two. Another student raised his hand, and the teacher called on him to answer the question.

Susan was completely lost. When the teacher asked her to discuss how the destruction of natural predators could disturb the food chain, she stammered that she didn't understand the question. Fortunately for Susan, the teacher then asked another student.

Felicia felt confident about contributing to the discussion. She volunteered several times, and the information and opinions she offered added to the discussion.

Comparing Passive and Active Thinking Methods

If you had to fold five hundred letters and stuff each letter into an envelope, you would find that your speed would increase as you learned a system for doing the job. Soon you would find that you could fold and stuff without really thinking about what you were doing. You could daydream, listen to music, talk to a friend, and still get the job done.

You can do the same thing when you study. You can read your history textbook without thinking about why the American colonial people wanted independence from England or how the Industrial Revolution influenced the politics and culture of Nineteenth Century Europe. The problem is that if you approach studying in the same way that you approach stuffing letters into envelopes, you are probably not going to do very well on the next history test.

In this chapter you will learn a reading method that will help you understand what you read. Once you understand what you read, you will discover that studying and remembering important information become much easier!

There are two methods that students generally use when they read. One method is called the **Passive Method**, and the other is called the **Active Thinking Method**. Students who use the Passive Method do not become involved in what they read. They simply go through the motions. Students who use the Active Thinking Method *do* become involved in what they read or study. These students understand and remember more. Compare the two methods below.

The Passive Method

1. Get through assignments as quickly as possible.

2. Look only for facts.

3. Hope that you will remember what you've read.

The Active Thinking Method

1. Think about what you are learning as you read.

2. Look for the main ideas.

3. After you are finished reading, review what you've learned so that you will remember important information.

Check here which method you use most often:

_____ The Passive Method _____ The Active Thinking Method

If you honestly feel that the Passive Method is the one you've been using up until now, then the material in this chapter is going to make your life a lot easier. You are going to learn how to use the Active Thinking Method!

The Active Thinking Method

The Six Steps to Active Thinking

1. Read the title.

2. Read the introduction.

3. Turn the main title and each subtitle into a question.

4. Read the material carefully.

5. Learn the meaning of difficult words used in the material.

6. Answer the questions about the main title and subtitles.

You will have an opportunity to practice the steps when you read the article "Newgrange—An Example of Ancient Science" on page 51. Do not read the article yet. For the present, simply read how to do the first five steps.

Step 1:	**Title**
Procedure:	Read the title of the article.
Why:	The title will usually tell you what the material is about.
Active Thinking:	Reading the title helps you focus on the general topic that is being presented.

Step 2:	**Introduction**
Procedure:	Carefully read the introduction to the material. The introduction is generally the first sentence of the article. Long articles will have an introductory paragraph or paragraphs.
Why:	The introduction provides important information about the subject of the article.
Active Thinking:	Reading the introduction helps you decide if you know anything about the subject. If you do not know anything about the subject, then your purpose in reading is to learn about the subject. If you do know something about the subject, your purpose in reading is to expand your knowledge on the subject.

Step 3:	**Question**
Procedure:	Turn the main title into a question. Turn each subtitle into a question. (In most textbooks subtitles are generally in bold print and introduce each section.)
	Use the six question words below to help you turn the title and subtitles into questions.

The six question words are

who	**where**
what	**why**
when	**how**

Why:	By asking yourself questions as you read, you are actively directing your attention to the key ideas in the material.
Active Thinking:	Involving yourself actively in what you are reading will help you understand and remember the material.

Step 4:   Read

Active Thinking:	Being aware that you are looking for the answers to the questions you asked in Step 3 will help you to read more effectively.

Step 5:   Definitions

Procedure:	As you read, find the meanings of the words you do not know. Words are sometimes defined in the text of the material you are reading. You may also be able to figure out the meaning of some words by seeing how they are used in the sentence. If there is a glossary at the end of the book, use it. Use a dictionary to look up any other unfamiliar words.
Why:	You must know what important words mean in order to understand what you are reading. If you don't know these meanings, you may miss the main point or idea. The key to being a smart student is understanding what you are studying. Remembering information is much easier when you know what it means.
Active Thinking:	Looking up the meanings of unfamiliar words may slow you down, but in the long run you will actually save studying time.

Step 6:   Answer

Procedure:	Answer the question about each subtitle after you have read that section. After you have read the entire article, answer the question about the main title.
Why:	If you can answer the question, then you have understood what you read.
Active Thinking:	When you think about what you read, you will be able to remember important information more easily.

Practice these Active Thinking steps as you read "Newgrange—An Example of Ancient Science."

In Steps 1 and 2 you will need to underline in the book. *Although you are asked to underline in this book, you probably are not allowed to underline or write in your school textbooks.*

Please note that the main title and the first subtitle have been turned into questions for you (Step 3). A sample answer to the question about the first subtitle is provided to demonstrate how to answer the questions (Step 6). Write out the rest of the questions and answers on your own. Refer to the six Active Thinking steps whenever you're not sure about what to do.

Applying the Active Thinking Method

Step 1: Underline title.

Step 2: Underline introduction.
(Hint: the introduction to the article is in boldface type.)

Step 3: Turn the main title into a question.
How is Newgrange an example of ancient science?

Turn each subtitle into a question.
Why is Newgrange a unique burial mound?

Step 4: Read each section.

Step 5: Find definitions. Look up the meanings of any unfamiliar words. *(Difficult words in this article are followed by stars. You will find their meanings in the glossary at the end of the book.)*

Step 6: Answer the question about the subtitle. (Step 3.)
Newgrange is a unique burial mound because it is so large and because it has remained dry for over 4000 years.

NEWGRANGE—AN EXAMPLE OF ANCIENT SCIENCE

Scientists who study ancient civilizations* can learn a great deal about the people who lived thousands of years ago. They do this by studying the monuments* that these people created. These scientists, called archeologists,* have learned that many ancient cultures were not as primitive* as people might think. In some cases, the people who lived long ago were capable* of creating and building monuments which are quite sophisticated and complex.

A UNIQUE BURIAL MOUND

An ancient structure which reveals a great deal about the people who lived thousands of years ago is called Newgrange.

Newgrange is an ancient burial mound. Located on the eastern side of Ireland, just north of Dublin, Newgrange was built around 2500 B.C. The structure consists of a huge mound of earth that is 42 feet high and 300 feet in diameter.* The entire mound covers more than an acre of land.

Newgrange is entered through a door on the south side of the mound. The door opens into a low, narrow passageway, 65 feet in length, which leads to the center of the mound.

At the center of the mound is a domed chamber. This chamber is 20 feet high and is made of stone. It was probably used as a burial place for the most important people of the tribe. Although the weather in Ireland can be very damp, the chamber is dry, even after four thousand years! The builders of Newgrange had discovered a method of construction that ensured that the center of the mound would stay dry.

Step 3:   Question.

_____

_____?

Step 4:   Read the section.

Step 5:   Find definitions.

Step 6:   Answer.

_____

_____

_____

_____

_____

_____

WATERPROOFING TECHNIQUES

The chamber in the center of the mound was constructed using a special process to keep it dry. This chamber resembles an upside-down bowl made of rough boulders. The builders started with a ring of these large stones, and then added one ring after another to the base. With each new layer of stones, the diameter of the circle became smaller and smaller, until finally, only a single capstone* was needed to form the roof. This process of building the chamber is called corbeling.

The outside edges of the stones were slanted downward, and narrow grooves were cut in the stones forming a drainage channel. The entire structure was covered with earth. When it rained, any water leaking through the earth to the stones below would run down the grooves to the base of the mound. Thus, water was kept from leaking into the chamber.

Step 3:   Question.

_____

_____?

Step 4:   Read the section.

Step 5:   Find definitions.

Step 6:   Answer.

_____

_____

_____

USING ARCHITECTURE AS A CALENDAR

A small rectangular hole above the door at the entrance of Newgrange puzzled archeologists for many years. At first, they thought that food was dropped through the hole into the passageway for the dead people who were buried in the mound. They later concluded that this theory was wrong.

One of the archeologists suspected that the hole had something to do with astronomy. He discovered that each year on December 21, the shortest day of the year, the first rays of the rising sun would strike the hole above the door. As the sun rose, its rays would shine through the hole and creep along the passageway until the entire chamber was finally illuminated.* After seventeen minutes, the light would quickly recede,* and the chamber would return to total darkness for another year.

A LASTING MONUMENT TO ANCIENT SCIENCE

The builders of Newgrange must have been keenly* aware of the sun and the changes in its position throughout the year. As primitive as they were, the people of ancient Ireland knew enough about engineering and astronomy to build a structure that was so perfectly in line with the sun that a chamber deep within it could be touched by the sun's rays one day each year. Perhaps the most amazing thing is that Newgrange still stands after thousands of years—as a monument to ancient science.

Step 3:   Question.

_____

_____

_____

_____

_____

Step 4:   Read the section.

Step 5:   Find definitions.

Step 6:   Answer.

_____

_____

_____

_____

Step 6:   Answer the question about the main title.

_____

_____

_____

_____

_____

Turn the page to compare your questions and answers with some sample questions and answers.

Sample Questions and Answers

Here are some sample questions and answers. Compare your questions and answers to these to make sure that you followed the steps correctly. Your questions and answers may not be exactly the same as these, but they should be similar.

Step 3:   **Question.** (See "Waterproofing Techniques.")

What were the waterproofing techniques?

Step 6:   **Answer.**

The builders of Newgrange used three waterproofing techniques: corbeling, or building the chamber in the shape of an upside-down bowl; slanting the outside edges of the stones downward; and cutting grooves into the stones so the water would run easily down the sides.

Step 3:   **Question.** (See "Using Architecture As a Calendar.")

How did they use architecture as a calendar?

Step 6:   **Answer.**

A hole above the entrance door allowed the sun to shine into the chamber on the shortest day of the year, December 21.

Step 3:   **Question.** (See "A Lasting Monument to Ancient Science.")

Why is Newgrange a lasting monument to ancient science?

Step 6:   **Answer.**

Even though the builders of Newgrange were primitive, they were able to build a scientific structure that has lasted for thousands of years.

Step 6:   Answer the question about the main title. (See page 51.)

Newgrange is an example of ancient science because knowledge of astronomy and engineering was needed to build the mound so that it was sturdy, so that it would stay dry, and so that it could act as a calendar.

Remembering the Steps

Review the six steps in the Active Thinking Method that you have just practiced. How can you remember the six steps? If you recall, in Chapter 2, we discussed four methods to help you remember information. Try each of the four methods and see which one works best for you.

Method 1:   **Write it down.**

Write down the six steps in the Active Thinking Method.

1. _____   4. _____

2. _____   5. _____

3. _____   6. _____

Method 2:   **Say it to yourself, over and over.**

Method 3:   **Create a picture in your mind.**

You might think of the Active Thinking Method as an hourglass. The first three steps in the method (Title, Introduction, and Question) act as a funnel leading to steps 4 (Read), 5 (Definitions), and 6 (Answer).

Active Thinking Method Hourglass

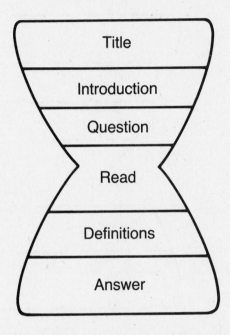

Like the sand which flows into the bottom of the hourglass and expands, so does your knowledge expand when you answer the questions.

Method 4:   **Make up a formula or sentence.**

To make up a formula, write down the first letter of each step.

T + I + Q + R + D + A

To make up a sentence, use each letter from the formula as the first letter in a new word.

First Example: Thinking **I**s **Q**uestioning; **R**ules **D**o **A**id.

Second Example: The **I**mpossible **Q**ueen **R**uns **D**own **A**lleys.

Make up your own sentence here.

Testing Yourself

Write down the Active Thinking Method Formula.

_____ + _____ + _____ + _____ + _____ + _____

Write down the Active Thinking Method sentence.

_____

Fill in the Active Thinking Method hourglass.

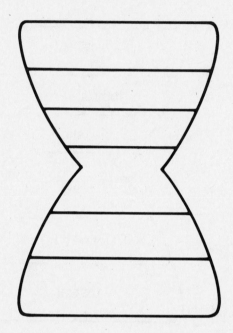

Match the correct definitions with the six steps in the Active Thinking Method. Draw a line from each step to its definition.

Title   The sentence or paragraph at the beginning of the article which tells what the article is about.

Introduction   A means of reviewing what you learned from the article.

Question   The place to find out what the article will be covering.

Read   The process of finding the information in the material in order to answer the questions.

Definitions   A means of using the title and subtitles to help you think about what the article will be covering.

Answer   The meanings of words used in the article.

Comparing Your Answers

Formula: $T + I + Q + R + D + A$

Sentence: **T**hinking **I**s **Q**uestioning; **R**ules **D**o **A**id.

Hourglass:

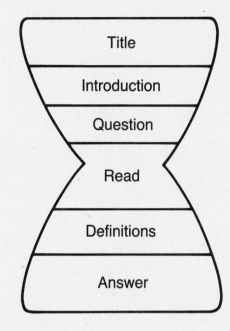

Title	The place to find out what the article will be covering.
Introduction	The sentence or paragraph at the beginning of the article which tells what the article is about.
Question	A means of using the title and subtitles to help you think about what the article will be covering.
Read	The process of finding the information in the material in order to answer the questions.
Definitions	The meanings of words used in the article.
Answer	A means of reviewing what you learned from the article.

What You Have Learned in This Chapter:

1. *How to read material so that you understand and remember it*

2. *How to use the Active Thinking Method*

3. *How to remember the six steps in the Active Thinking Method*

CHAPTER 6
A Review of the Active Thinking Method

Time Required: Approximately 90 Minutes

In this chapter you will review the six steps
in the Active Thinking Method.

Reviewing the Six Steps

You are now going to practice the new study skills you learned in the last chapter. You will find another, slightly longer article below. Follow the six steps in the Active Thinking Method.

1. Title
2. Introduction
3. Question

4. Read
5. Definitions
6. Answer

Remember the formula: **T + I + Q + R + D + A** (**T**hinking **I**s **Q**uestioning; **R**ules **D**o **A**id).

Do the first three steps before you read the entire article. Write your questions and answers in the blanks provided. Please note that certain words that may be unfamiliar to you are starred. The definitions of these words can be found in the glossary at the back of the book. It is most important that you know the meanings of these words as you read so that you will be able to understand the article.

Practicing the Active Thinking Method

Step 1: Underline title.

Step 2: Underline introduction.

Step 3: Turn the main title into a question.
Who was the lady Pharaoh of Egypt and what did she do?

Turn each subtitle into a question.
Who was Thutmose I?

Step 4: Read each section.

Step 5: Find definitions.

Look up the meanings of any unfamiliar words.
(Difficult words in this article are followed by stars. You will find their meanings in the glossary at the end of the book.)

Step 6: Answer the question about the subtitle.
Thutmose I was the Pharaoh of Egypt. He had two children, Hatshepsut and Thutmose II. He was worried about who would rule after him.

Step 3: Question.

_____ ?

Step 4: Read the section.

Step 5: Definitions.

Step 6: Answer.

_____

_____

_____

_____

THE LADY PHARAOH OF EGYPT

Three thousand five hundred (3500) years ago, there lived a courageous woman named Hatshepsut (Hat'-shep-sut). She not only dared to declare herself queen of Egypt but also had the courage to make herself Pharaoh.★

THUTMOSE I

Hatshepsut was born around 1503 B.C. She was the daughter of Thutmose I (Thut'-mōs), the Pharaoh of Egypt, and his wife Amose (O'-mōs). As a child, Hatshepsut adored her father. He was a mighty warrior who had kept Egypt safe from outside invaders and had helped the country become prosperous.★

As Thutmose I grew older, he began to worry about who would rule over the land he loved so much. He had one son, Thutmose II, who was Hatshepsut's half brother. But Thutmose II was weak, somewhat lazy, and not too interested in learning how to run the government.

CROWN PRINCE

Hatshepsut, unlike her brother, was a bundle of energy! She was fascinated with government and with the responsibilities of leadership. Because of these qualities, Thutmose I had her educated as a son. Not only did she learn to read and write, but she also excelled★ in the soldier's arts: horseback riding, hunting, throwing spears, and driving chariots.

Thutmose I wanted the people to accept Hatshepsut as their ruler. When he declared that Hatshepsut would be his successor,★ he named her the "crown prince." He then took her on a goodwill tour of Egypt in order to present her to his people.

Everywhere that Hatshepsut went, the people spoke of her radiant* beauty. They recognized her authority and her ability. The trip was a huge success. Hatshepsut returned home more convinced than ever that she was destined* to rule Egypt.

Step 3:   Question.

_____?

Step 4:   Read the section.

Step 5:   Definitions.

Step 6:   Answer.

_____

_____

_____

_____

_____

THUTMOSE II

Unfortunately, when Thutmose I died, Hatshepsut discovered that she did not have enough power to become Pharaoh. Her brother Thutmose II was named Pharaoh, and Hatshepsut was forced to marry him. (In Egypt during this period, it was not unusual for royal half brothers and sisters to marry.) Although Thutmose II held the title of Pharaoh, it was Hatshepsut who actually governed the country.

Step 3:   Question.

_____?

Step 4:   Read the section.

Step 5:   Definitions.

Step 6:   Answer.

_____

_____

_____

NUBIA

The authority of the new Pharaoh and his bride was quickly challenged. There was an uprising in Nubia, a neighboring country under Egypt's rule. Most historians agree that Hatshepsut herself led her army into a victorious* battle in which the Nubians were crushed, and all of their chiefs were captured and killed.

Step 3:   Question.

_____

_____?

Step 4:   Read the section.

Step 5:   Definitions.

Step 6:   Answer.

_____

_____

_____

_____

HATSHEPSUT BECOMES PHARAOH

Thutmose II and Hatshepsut had two daughters but no sons. Because Pharaohs often had many wives during this period, Thutmose II did have a son, named Thutmose III, by a lesser wife. Thutmose III was a strong, healthy child who resembled his grandfather more than his weak father, Thutmose II.

Thutmose II lived for only a few more years. When he died, it was assumed* that Hatshepsut and Thutmose III would rule together until Thutmose III was old enough to rule alone. Hatshepsut had other plans. Realizing that Thutmose III was too young to object, Hatshepsut had herself declared the only Pharaoh. She took complete control of the country and placed her friends and advisors in important positions. To strengthen her claim to the throne, she often wore men's clothing. She would wear a helmet and even a false beard like the false beards that had been worn by earlier Pharaohs. Because of her efforts to act and dress like a man, her subjects actually referred to her as "His Majesty."

Step 3:   Question.

_____

_____?

Step 4:   Read the section.

Step 5:   Definitions.

Step 6:   Answer.

_____

_____

BUILDING PROJECTS

Hatshepsut's reign* was a time of peace and prosperity.* Because her family had established a tradition* of building great monuments,* Hatshepsut devoted a good deal of time and money to her building projects. She rebuilt many of the ruined temples in her country. Her personal architect designed a mortuary* temple for her which even today is considered to be one of the most beautiful in Egypt.

Hatshepsut also commissioned*

_____

_____

_____

two huge obelisks* to be built. An obelisk is a huge, four-sided stone pillar which can stand over 50 feet high and comes to a point at the top. Each obelisk was cut out of a single piece of rock, floated down the Nile River, and then carefully raised into place. This entire process took only seven months!

Hatshepsut wanted the obelisks to be completely covered with gold so they would reflect the rays of the rising sun. The cost for doing this, however, was too great. Hatshepsut had to content herself with covering only the tips of the obelisks with gold. Today, one of these obelisks still stands and is the tallest monument in Egypt.

Step 3:   Question.

_____

_____ ?

Step 4:   Read the section.

Step 5:   Definitions.

Step 6:   Answer.

_____

_____

_____

_____

_____

EXPEDITION TO PUNT

Perhaps Hatshepsut's greatest accomplishment was the expedition* she sent to the land of Punt. As a child, Hatshepsut had heard countless stories about how her ancestors had traded with the people of that country. But the knowledge of the trade routes had been lost, and no one knew where the land of Punt was located.

Hatshepsut was determined to open trade once again with the people of Punt. She outfitted* five ships with her most capable* sailors. She sent them off with instructions to find the land of Punt.

The ships were gone for three years. Finally, they returned laden* with fabulous treasures. These treasures included myrrh* trees, monkeys and baboons, panther skins, ebony,* ivory, gold, and other precious objects. As a result of this expedition, trade was reopened between the two countries, and Egypt acquired great wealth.

Step 3:   Question.

_____

_____ ?

Step 4:   Read the section.

Step 5:   Definitions.

Step 6:   Answer.

_____

_____

_____

_____

_____

_____

THUTMOSE III GAINS CONTROL

The people of Egypt grew wealthy under Hatshepsut's rule. Despite this prosperity, a deadly struggle was beginning. Thutmose III was growing up and wanted the power that he thought was rightfully his. Hatshepsut, however, was too strong to be overthrown.* So Thutmose III and some of his priests designed a plan to undermine* her.

One day, during the daily ceremony in the temple, the priests were carrying the statue of the Egyptian god Amun. Suddenly the statue seemed to be searching for someone. When it reached the place where Thutmose was standing, the statue stopped abruptly and bowed low before him. The priests explained to the people that the god had chosen Thutmose III to be their king.

This incident marked the beginning of Hatshepsut's decline.* Thutmose III's power grew stronger and stronger, and he began to gain more influence in the country. Although it is known that he took over the throne, it is not clear how he finally did so.

Did Hatshepsut die of natural causes? Or was she murdered or simply overthrown? Most of the hieroglyphics* that tell the story of Hatshepsut have been scratched out. Perhaps Thutmose III had this done in order to erase all mention of the woman who had kept him from the throne for so long.

It is fairly certain that Hatshepsut died in the year 1482 B.C. She left behind a healthy, happy, and wealthy country. In becoming Pharaoh of Egypt, she had accomplished what no woman before her had done. Because of these achievements, Hatshepsut must be considered one of the most extraordinary women in history.

Step 6:   Answer the question from the main title. (See page 60.)

_____

_____

_____

_____

Sample Questions and Answers

Below you will find examples of how a student might have used the Active Thinking Method as he or she read the article "The Lady Pharaoh of Egypt." Compare these answers with yours. Although your answers will not be exactly like those modeled below, they should be similar.

Step 1:   Underline the title.

The Lady Pharaoh of Egypt

Step 2:   Underline the introduction.

Three thousand five hundred (3500) years ago, there lived a courageous woman named Hatshepsut. She not only dared to declare herself queen of Egypt but also had the courage to make herself Pharaoh.

Step 3:   Turn the main title into a question.

Who was the lady Pharaoh of Egypt and **what** did she do?

Step 3:   Turn each subtitle into a question.

Who was Thutmose I?

Step 6:   Answer.

Thutmose I was the Pharaoh of Egypt. He had two children, Hatshepsut and Thutmose II. He was worried about who would rule after him.

Step 3:   **Why** was Hatshepsut named the "crown prince"?

Step 6:   Hatshepsut was named the "crown prince" because her father wanted her, and not her brother, to rule after him.

Step 3:   **What** did Thutmose II do?

Step 6:   He became Pharaoh after Thutmose I because Hatshepsut didn't have enough power to become Pharaoh. It was Hatshepsut who really ruled the country.

Step 3:   **What** happened in Nubia?

Step 6:   Nubia revolted against Egypt. Hatshepsut led the Egyptian army to crush the revolt.

Step 3:   **How** did Hatshepsut become Pharaoh?

Step 6:   When Thutmose II died, Hatshepsut was supposed to rule with Thutmose III. She was able to take over complete control because Thutmose III was too young to rule the country.

Step 3:   **What** were her building projects?

Step 6:   She rebuilt ruined temples and built a mortuary temple for herself. She also built two obelisks tipped with gold.

Step 3:   **What** was the expedition to Punt?

Step 6:   Hatshepsut sent five ships to find the country of Punt. The ships returned after three years with treasures. The expedition reopened trade between the two countries and brought Egypt great wealth.

Step 3:   **How** did Thutmose III gain control?

Thutmose and his priests thought of a plan to undermine Hatshepsut. In the temple, the priests were carrying a statue of the god Amun. When the statue was in front of Thutmose, it bowed. The people believed that this meant that the god wanted Thutmose III to be the Pharaoh.

Step 6:   Answer the question from the main title.
(Who was the lady Pharaoh of Egypt and what did she do?)

Hatshepsut was the lady Pharaoh of Egypt. She was the first woman to rule Egypt alone. She rebuilt temples, built two obelisks, reopened trade with Punt, and brought peace and prosperity to Egypt.

Testing Yourself

See how well you remember the six steps you used in Chapters 5 and 6. Write down the Active Thinking Method Formula.

_____ + _____ + _____ + _____ + _____ + _____

Write down the Active Thinking Method sentence.

_____

Fill in the Active Thinking Method hourglass.

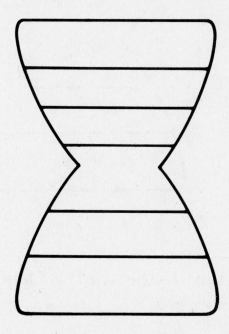

Comparing Your Answers

Formula: T + I + Q + R + D + A

Sentence: **T**hinking **I**s **Q**uestioning; **R**ules **D**o **A**id.

Hourglass:

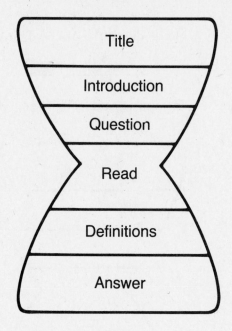

Title
Introduction
Question
Read
Definitions
Answer

What You Have Learned in This Chapter:

1. *How to read material so that you understand and remember it*

2. *How to use the Active Thinking Method*

3. *How to remember the six steps in the Active Thinking Method*

CHAPTER 7
Taking Notes

Time Required: Approximately 90 Minutes

In this chapter you will learn how to take notes by identifying

1. the main ideas in an article

2. the important details in an article

3. the point of an article

A Typical History Assignment

Ms. Rossi assigned pages 345–358 in the history textbook to be read for homework. She instructed the students to read the material carefully so that they would be ready for the class discussion the next day.

Susan read the material during a half hour break between two of her favorite TV programs. She was quite proud of herself for completing the assignment.

John had talked with Felicia during the week about the study method she had learned from her older sister. Felicia told him that the method helped her understand what she read. John decided to try Felicia's system. It took John an hour to complete the assignment. John felt confident that he understood the material and that he would be able to participate in a class discussion.

Felicia also used her sister's Active Thinking Method to do her homework. It took her approximately one hour to complete the assignment. When she had finished, she did something else. *Felicia took notes.*

Felicia wrote down every bit of information that might be important. Her notes were five pages long and were written in complete sentences. Because the assignment took two and a half hours, she had to stay up till 11:30 in order to finish her other homework.

Ms. Rossi surprised her students the next day with a quiz covering the assigned reading. Susan received a **C** on the quiz. "It's pretty easy to pass if you read the assignment," she thought to herself. "No more **D**'s and **F**'s for me!"

John received a **B +** . He was amazed at how much of the material he had been able to recall.

Felicia breezed through the quiz with an **A**. She was delighted with her grade, but she wasn't sure she could afford to spend so much time on one assignment.

While most students want to get **A**'s, few students have the time or the desire to spend two and a half hours on one assignment. *Taking notes does not have to take an endless amount of time.* With a good note-taking system, Felicia could have saved an hour of homework time and still gotten an **A**.

This chapter will teach you how to take notes efficiently and effectively. Compare the two lists below to see the difference taking notes can make.

Studying without notes makes it	**Studying with notes makes it**
1. difficult to identify important information	1. easier to identify important information
2. difficult to understand important information	2. easier to understand important information
3. difficult to remember important information	3. easier to remember important information
4. difficult to review for exams	4. easier to review for exams

Two Steps to Taking Good Notes

There are two basic steps in the note-taking process.

1. Writing down the **main ideas**

2. Writing down the **details**

You will practice these two steps by taking notes on an article that you have already read, "Newgrange—An Example of Ancient Science."

The Note-Taking System

Read through the procedure for the **Note-Taking System**. Do not worry about remembering all of the information. You will have plenty of opportunity to practice each step.

Step 1:   **Main Ideas**

Procedure: Write down the **main ideas** of the article. In "Newgrange—An Example of Ancient Science," as in most articles and textbooks, the main ideas can be found in the subheadings.

Why: The main ideas represent the most important information in the article. The main ideas provide the frame that holds the information together.

Organization: The main ideas should be written next to the left-hand margin on your note paper. Do not write in complete sentences. Just copy the subheadings from the article. (See sample page of notes on page 76.)

Step 2:   **Details**

Procedure: Write down the important **details** that support each main idea. As you read each section of the article, you must decide which are the most important details that will help you understand and remember the main ideas.

Why: The details provide additional information about the main ideas. If the main ideas are like a frame or the skeleton of the body, the details are like the flesh which fills out the skeleton to make a whole body. Without the details you do not have a complete understanding of each main idea.

Organization: The details should be indented about one inch from the left-hand margin. They should be listed one under the other. Do not write in complete sentences. Just include the key words or phrases. Make sure to include enough details so that you will understand your notes when you look back through them. (See sample notes on page 76.)

Applying the Note-Taking System

The article "Newgrange—An Example of Ancient Science" is reprinted here. As you reread the article, write your notes on the page facing the article.

   Sample notes covering the first two paragraphs have already been written for you. As you look at these sample notes, you can see that

- the main idea from the introduction has been written next to the left-hand margin

- the first main idea in the body of the article has been written next to the left-hand margin (note that the main idea has been copied directly from subtitle 1)

- the important details from the first paragraph of the first section have been placed under the main idea

Continue reading the article and taking notes, using the sample notes as a model. *Notice that important details have been underlined.* This has been done to help you recognize the information that should be included in your notes.

- Write the main ideas and the details in the spaces.

- Use as few words as possible. Do not write in complete sentences.

NEWGRANGE—AN EXAMPLE OF ANCIENT SCIENCE

Scientists who study ancient civilizations can learn a great deal about the people who lived thousands of years ago. They do this by studying the monuments that these people created. These scientists, called archeologists, have learned that many ancient cultures were not as primitive as people might think. In some cases, the people who lived long ago were capable of creating and building monuments which are quite sophisticated and complex.

A Unique Burial Mound

An ancient structure which reveals a great deal about the people who lived thousands of years ago is called Newgrange. Newgrange is an ancient burial mound. Located on the eastern side of Ireland, just north of Dublin, Newgrange was built around 2500 B.C. The structure consists of a huge mound of earth that is 42 feet high and 300 feet in diameter. The entire mound covers more than an acre of land.

Newgrange is entered through a door on the south side of the mound. The door opens into a low, narrow passageway, 65 feet in length, which leads to the center of the mound.

At the center of the mound is a domed chamber. This chamber is 20 feet high and is made of stone. It was probably used as a burial place for the most important people of the tribe. Although the weather in Ireland can be very damp, the chamber is dry, even after 4000 years! The builders of Newgrange had discovered a method of construction that ensured that the center of the mound would stay dry.

Waterproofing Techniques

The chamber in the center of the mound was constructed using a special process to keep it dry. This chamber resembles an upside-down bowl made of rough boulders. The builders started with a ring of these large stones, and then added one ring after another to the base. With each new layer of stones, the diameter of the circle became smaller and smaller, until finally, only a single capstone was needed to form the roof. This process of building the chamber is called corbeling.

The outside edges of the stones were slanted downward, and narrow grooves were cut in the stones forming a drainage channel. The entire structure was covered with earth. When it rained, any water leaking through the earth to the stones below would run down the grooves to the base of the mound. Thus, water was kept from leaking into the chamber.

Newgrange—An Example of Ancient Science

Step 1:   Main Idea (from the introduction) <u>Archeologists discover that some</u>

<u>ancient people were not as primitive as believed.</u>

Step 1:   Main Idea (the first subtitle)

<u>Unique Burial Mound</u>

Step 2:   Details (from the first section)

• <u>Newgrange—burial mound in Ireland</u>

• <u>built 2500 B.C.</u>

• <u>mound: 42 ft high, 300 ft diameter, covers 1 acre</u>

• <u>door on south side</u>

• <u>low, narrow passageway, 65 ft long, leads to center</u>

Step 1:   Main Idea (the second subtitle)

_____

Step 2:   Details (from the second section)

_____

_____

_____

_____

_____

_____

Step 1:   Main Idea (the third subtitle)

_____

Step 2:   Details (from the third subtitle)

_____

_____

Using Architecture As a Calendar

A small rectangular hole above the door at the entrance of Newgrange puzzled archeologists for many years. At first, they thought that food was dropped through the hole into the passageway for the dead people who were buried in the mound. They later concluded that this theory was wrong.

One of the archeologists suspected that the hole had something to do with astronomy. He discovered that each year on December 21, the shortest day of the year, the first rays of the rising sun would strike the hole above the door. As the sun rose, its rays would shine through the hole and creep along the passageway until the entire chamber was finally illuminated. After seventeen minutes, the light would quickly recede, and the chamber would return to total darkness for another year.

A Lasting Monument to Ancient Science

The builders of Newgrange must have been keenly aware of the sun and the changes in its position throughout the year. As primitive as they were, the people of ancient Ireland knew enough about engineering and astronomy to build a structure that was so perfectly in line with the sun that a chamber hidden 65 feet within it could be touched by the sun's rays one day each year. Perhaps the most amazing thing is that Newgrange still stands after thousands of years—as a monument to ancient science.

_____

_____

_____

_____

_____

_____

_____

_____

_____

Step 1:   Main Idea (the fourth subtitle)

_____

Step 2:   Details (from the fourth section)

_____

_____

_____

_____

_____

_____

_____

_____

_____

Comparing Notes

Below you will find a sample page of notes that have been taken from the article "Newgrange—An Example of Ancient Science." Compare your notes with these. Yours should be almost the same. If they are not, make the necessary corrections in your notes. Look back through the article to see what information you didn't include.

Newgrange—An Example of Ancient Science

Step 1:   Archeologists discover that some ancient people were not as primitive as believed.

Step 1:   <u>Unique Burial Mound</u>

Step 2:
- Newgrange—burial mound in Ireland
- built 2500 B.C.
- mound—42 ft high, 300 ft diameter, covers 1 acre
- door on south side
- low, narrow passageway, 65 ft long, leads to center
- center—domed stone chamber, 20 ft high, still dry today

Step 1:   <u>Waterproofing Techniques</u>

Step 2:
- chamber resembles upside-down bowl
- ring of stones
- built one ring on top of another
- stone rings become smaller going up
- *capstone* (top stone) formed roof
- building process called *corbeling*
- outside edges of stones slanted down
- narrow grooves cut in stone
- chamber and passageway covered with earth

Step 1:   <u>Using Architecture As a Calendar</u>

Step 2:
- small rectangular hole above door
- December 21—shortest day of year
- sun's rays shine through hole
- sun illuminates (lights up) chamber for 17 minutes
- chamber dark rest of year

Step 1:   <u>Lasting Monument to Ancient Science</u>

Step 2:   • builders of Newgrange aware that sun changes position

• knew enough about engineering and astronomy to line up mound with sun

• Newgrange still standing

The Note-Taking Triangle

To help you understand and remember the Active Thinking Method that you learned in Chapter 5, it was suggested that you picture an hourglass that consists of six levels (Title, Introduction, Question, Read, Definitions, Answer).

To help you understand and remember the Note-Taking System, we suggest that you picture an upside-down triangle that consists of three levels. Look at the picture below. You will see an inverted triangle. The top level consists of the main ideas, and the second level consists of the details. The bottom section is called the **point**. You will now learn how to figure out the point of what you have read.

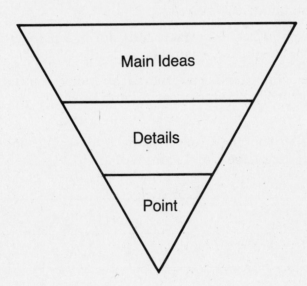

Getting the Point

Look at the illustration of the inverted triangle on page 77. The main ideas and the details lead the reader to the point being made by the author. When taking notes, you start with the main ideas. You then expand your knowledge about the main ideas by writing down the details. This process helps reinforce your memory and your understanding of what you have read.

The third step in note-taking is to summarize the main ideas. This summarization is the point. If you can express the point of an article in your own words, you will be able to

1. understand the information

2. remember the information

3. do better on tests

You will now learn the third step in the Note-Taking System.

Step 3:	**Point**
Procedure:	Write down the point of the material you have read. The point represents the unifying idea or ideas that the author wants to communicate to the readers.
Why:	The point ties all the facts and information together. It is generally found in the conclusion or summary.
Organization:	The point should be written at the end of your notes next to the left-hand margin of your note paper.

Practicing Getting the Point

Review your notes and write down the point that the author is making in "Newgrange—An Example of Ancient Science."

_____

_____

_____

_____

_____

_____

Compare your summary of the point with the sample below. Your words may be different, but the information should be the same. *Don't be discouraged if you need to rewrite or add to your summary*. With practice, your ability to express the point of what you have read will improve!

Step 3:   **Point**

Newgrange proves that ancient people were not primitive in all ways. They were able to build a monument that was waterproof, functioned as a simple calendar, and was sturdy enough to remain standing for thousands of years.

Testing Yourself

Write down the three steps in the Note-Taking System.

1. _____

2. _____

3. _____

Say aloud the three steps in the Note-Taking System.

Make up a formula using the first letter in each step.

_____ + _____ + _____

Make up a sentence with the first letter of each word.

_____

Fill in the inverted triangle with the three steps.

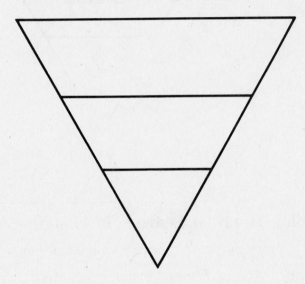

Comparing Your Answers

Three Steps in the Note-Taking System:

1. Main Ideas
2. Details
3. Point

Formula:

MI   +   D   +   P

Sentence (sample): MI (My) Dog Plays

Triangle:

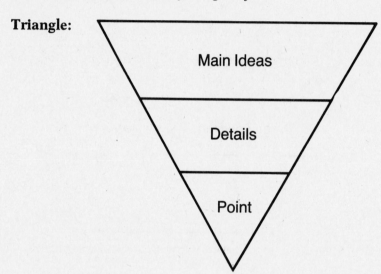

What You Have Learned in This Chapter:

1. *How to take notes in an easy-to-read format*
2. *How to identify the main idea in an article*
3. *How to identify the important details in an article*
4. *How to identify the point of an article*

CHAPTER 8
A Review of the Note-Taking System

Time Required: Approximately 90 Minutes

In this chapter you will review the three steps
that you learned in Chapter 7.

Practicing the Note-Taking System

You are now going to practice on your own the note-taking skills you learned in the last chapter. On the next page you will find a reprint of the article "The Lady Pharaoh of Egypt," which you read in Chapter 6. Reread the article to refresh your memory.

Many students find it helpful to underline important details in their books as they read. You may not be allowed to underline in your school textbooks, but you may want to try underlining in this book to see if it helps you understand and remember the information.

As you reread the article "The Lady Pharaoh of Egypt," take notes. Write your notes on the specially designed pages that you will find opposite each section of the text. These pages have been set up to help you master the Note-Taking System. Be sure to follow the three steps in the Note-Taking System.

1. Main ideas

2. Details

3. Point

Remember:

1. Write each main idea next to the left-hand margin.
2. Use the subtitles as the main ideas.
3. Set up your paper so that the details are listed under each main idea.
4. Use as few words as possible.

THE LADY PHARAOH OF EGYPT

Three thousand five hundred (3500) years ago, there lived a courageous woman named Hatshepsut (Hat'-shep-sut). She not only dared to declare herself queen of Egypt but also had the courage to make herself Pharaoh.

Thutmose I

Hatshepsut was born around 1503 B.C. She was the daughter of Thutmose I (Thut'-mōs), the Pharaoh of Egypt, and his wife Amose (O'-mōs). As a child, Hatshepsut adored her father. He was a mighty warrior who had kept Egypt safe from outside invaders and had helped the country become prosperous.

As Thutmose I grew older, he began to worry about who would rule over the land he loved so much. He had one son, Thutmose II, who was Hatshepsut's half brother. But Thutmose II was weak, somewhat lazy, and not too interested in learning how to run the government.

Crown Prince

Hatshepsut, unlike her brother, was a bundle of energy! She was fascinated with government and with the responsibilities of leadership. Because of these qualities, Thutmose I had her educated as a son. Not only did she learn to read and write, but she also excelled in the soldier's arts: horseback riding, hunting, throwing spears, and driving chariots.

Thutmose I wanted the people to accept Hatshepsut as their ruler. When he declared that Hatshepsut would be his successor, he named her the "crown prince." He then took her on a goodwill tour of Egypt in order to present her to his people.

Everywhere that Hatshepsut went, the people spoke of her radiant beauty. They recognized her authority and her ability. The trip was a huge success. Hatshepsut returned home more convinced than ever that she was destined to rule Egypt.

continued on page 84

Notes _____

Step 1:   Main Idea (from the introduction)

_____

Step 1:   Main Idea (the first subtitle)

_____

Step 2:   Details (from the first section)

_____

_____

_____

_____

_____

_____

_____

Step 1:   Main Idea (the second subtitle)

_____

Step 2:   Details (from the second section)

_____

_____

_____

_____

_____

_____

_____

Thutmose II

Unfortunately, when Thutmose I died, Hatshepsut discovered that she did not have enough power to become Pharaoh. Her brother Thutmose II was named Pharaoh, and Hatshepsut was forced to marry him. (In Egypt during this period, it was not unusual for royal half brothers and sisters to marry.) Although Thutmose II held the title of Pharaoh, it was Hatshepsut who actually governed the country.

Nubia

The authority of the new Pharaoh and his bride was quickly challenged. There was an uprising in Nubia, a neighboring country under Egypt's rule. Most historians agree that Hatshepsut herself led her army into a victorious battle in which the Nubians were crushed, and all of their chiefs were captured and killed.

Hatshepsut Becomes Pharaoh

Thutmose II and Hatshepsut had two daughters but no sons. Because Pharaohs often had many wives during this period, Thutmose II did have a son, named Thutmose III, by a lesser wife. Thutmose III was a strong, healthy child who resembled his grandfather more than his weak father, Thutmose II.

Thutmose II lived for only a few more years. When he died, it was assumed that Hatshepsut and Thutmose III would rule together until Thutmose III was old enough to rule alone. Hatshepsut had other plans. Realizing that Thutmose III was too young to object, Hatshepsut had herself declared the only Pharaoh. She took complete control of the country and placed her friends and advisors in important positions. To strengthen her claim to the throne, she often wore men's clothing. She would wear a helmet and even a false beard like the false beards that had been worn by earlier Pharaohs. Because of her efforts to act and dress like a man, her subjects actually referred to her as "His Majesty."

continued on page 86

Notes _____

Step 1:   Main Idea (the third subtitle)

_____

Step 2:   Details (from the third section)

_____

_____

_____

_____

_____

_____

Step 1:   Main Idea (the fourth subtitle)

_____

Step 2:   Details (from the fourth section)

_____

_____

_____

Step 1:   Main Idea (the fifth subtitle)

_____

Step 2:   Details (from the fifth section)

_____

_____

_____

_____

_____

Building Projects

Hatshepsut's reign was a time of peace and prosperity. Because her family had established a tradition of building great monuments, Hatshepsut devoted a good deal of time and money to her building projects. She rebuilt many of the ruined temples in her country. Her personal architect designed a mortuary temple for her which even today is considered to be one of the most beautiful in Egypt.

Hatshepsut also commissioned two huge obelisks to be built. An obelisk is a huge, four-sided stone pillar which can stand over fifty feet high and comes to a point at the top. Each obelisk was cut out of a single piece of rock, floated down the Nile River, and then carefully raised into place. This entire process took only seven months!

Hatshepsut wanted the obelisks to be completely covered with gold so they would reflect the rays of the rising sun. The cost for doing this, however, was too great. Hatshepsut had to content herself with covering only the tips of the obelisks with gold. Today, one of these obelisks still stands and is the tallest monument in Egypt.

Expedition to Punt

Perhaps Hatshepsut's greatest accomplishment was the expedition she sent to the land of Punt. As a child, Hatshepsut had heard countless stories about how her ancestors had traded with the people of that country. But the knowledge of the trade routes had been lost, and no one knew where the land of Punt was located.

Hatshepsut was determined to open trade once again with the people of Punt. She outfitted five ships with her most capable sailors. She sent them off with instructions to find the land of Punt.

The ships were gone for three years. Finally, they returned laden with fabulous treasures. These treasures included myrrh trees, monkeys and baboons, panther skins, ebony, ivory, gold, and other precious objects. As a result of this expedition, trade was reopened between the two countries, and Egypt acquired great wealth.

continued on page 88

Notes _____

Step 1:   Main Idea (the sixth subtitle)

_____

Step 2:   Details (from the sixth section) _____

_____

_____

_____

_____

_____

_____

_____

Step 1:   Main Idea (the seventh subtitle)

_____

Step 2:   Details (from the seventh section)

_____

_____

_____

_____

_____

_____

_____

_____

Thutmose III Gains Control

The people of Egypt grew wealthy under Hatshepsut's rule. Despite this prosperity, a deadly struggle was beginning. Thutmose III was growing up and wanted the power that he thought was rightfully his. Hatshepsut, however, was too strong to be overthrown. So Thutmose III and some of his priests designed a plan to undermine her.

One day, during the daily ceremony in the temple, the priests were carrying the statue of the Egyptian god Amun. Suddenly the statue seemed to be searching for someone. When it reached the place where Thutmose was standing, the statue stopped abruptly and bowed low before him. The priests explained to the people that the god had chosen Thutmose III to be their king.

This incident marked the beginning of Hatshepsut's decline. Thutmose III's power grew stronger and stronger, and he began to gain more influence in the country. Although it is known that he took over the throne, it is not clear how he finally did so.

Did Hatshepsut die of natural causes? Or was she murdered or simply overthrown? Most of the hieroglyphics that tell the story of Hatshepsut have been scratched out. Perhaps Thutmose III had this done in order to erase all mention of the woman who had kept him from the throne for so long.

It is fairly certain that Hatshepsut died in the year 1482 B.C. She left behind a healthy, happy, and wealthy country. In becoming Pharaoh of Egypt, she had accomplished what no woman before her had done. Because of these achievements, Hatshepsut must be considered one of the most extraordinary women in history.

Notes _____

Step 1:   Main Idea (the eighth subtitle)

_____

Step 2:   Details (from the eighth section)

_____

_____

_____

_____

_____

_____

_____

Step 3:   Point (Summarize the main ideas in your own words.)

_____

_____

_____

_____

_____

_____

_____

_____

_____

Comparing Notes

Here are sample notes from the article "The Lady Pharaoh of Egypt." Compare your notes with these. Yours should be almost the same. If they are not, make the necessary corrections in your notes. Look back in the article to find any information you didn't include.

Sample Notes

Step 1.   Hatshepsut—courageous Pharaoh of Egypt

Step 1.   <u>Thutmose I</u>
Step 2.   • Hat. born 1503 B.C.

• father Thutmose I—Pharaoh of Egypt, mighty warrior

• he worried about who would follow him

• Thutmose II—her half brother—lazy, weak

Step 1.   <u>Crown Prince</u>
Step 2.   • Hatshepsut educated as son

• Thutmose I wanted Hatshepsut to be next ruler

• named her "crown prince"

• goodwill tour of Egypt—huge success

Step 1.   <u>Thutmose II</u>
Step 2.   • Thut. I died

• Hat. didn't have enough power

• married Thut. II—he was Pharaoh

• she really governed

Step 1.   <u>Nubia</u>
Step 2.   • neighboring country

• uprising

• Hat. led army

• defeated Nubians

Step 1.   <u>Hat. Becomes Pharaoh</u>
Step 2.   • Hat. and Thut. II had 2 daughters

• Thut. II had son, Thut. III, by lesser wife—similar to Thut. I—strong

• Thut. II died

• Hat. and Thut. III supposed to rule together

• Hat. had herself declared only Pharaoh

- wore men's clothing
- was called "His Majesty"

Step 1. <u>Building Projects</u>

Step 2.
- peace and prosperity
- rebuilt ruined temples
- mortuary temple built for Hat.
- 2 obelisks—4-sided stone pillar, over 50 ft tall, comes to point at top
- 7 months to build
- tips covered w/*gold to reflect sun's rays
- 1 still stands—tallest monument in Egypt

*w/ is the abbreviation for the word "with."

Step 1. <u>Expedition to Punt</u>

Step 2.
- as child, Hat. had heard about country
- knowledge of trade routes lost
- Hat. sent five ships to find Punt
- gone 3 years
- returned with treasures
- reopened trade w/Punt
- brought wealth to Egypt

Step 1. <u>Thutmose III Gains Control</u>

Step 2.
- Thut. III wanted power
- designed plan w/priests
- in temple, priests carrying statue of god Amun made statue bow before Thut. III—said Thut. III chosen by god to be king
- beginning of Hat.'s decline
- Thut. III took control—not known how
- hieroglyphics about Hat. scratched out—maybe by Thut. III
- Hat. died 1482 B.C.
- left happy, healthy, wealthy country
- no other woman had done what she did

Step 3.   **Point:** Hatshepsut was the first woman Pharaoh of Egypt. She accomplished many things: rebuilt temples, had 2 obelisks built, and reopened trade with Punt. She made Egypt happy, healthy, and wealthy.

Testing Yourself

Write down the three steps in the Note-Taking System.

1. _____

2. _____

3. _____

Say aloud the three steps in the Note-Taking System.

Make up a formula using the first letter in each step.

_____ + _____ + _____

Make up a sentence with the first letter of each word.

_____

Fill in the inverted triangle with the three steps.

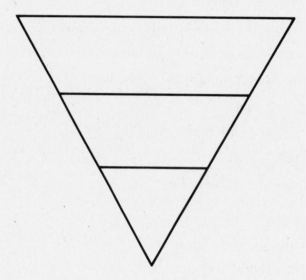

Comparing Your Answers

Three Steps in Note-Taking:

1. Main Ideas
2. Details
3. Point

Formula:

MI + D + P

Sentence:

MI (My) Dog Plays

Inverted Triangle:

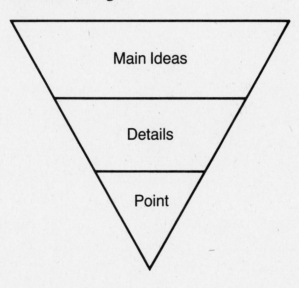

What You Have Learned in This Chapter:

1. *How to take notes in an easy-to-read format*
2. *How to identify the main ideas in an article*
3. *How to identify important details in an article*
4. *How to identify the point of an article*

CHAPTER 9
Taking Tests

Time Required: Approximately 45 Minutes

In this chapter you will learn

1. how the Active Thinking Method and the Note-Taking System can help you prepare for tests

2. how to overcome your fear of tests

Fear of Tests

Felicia felt the knot in her stomach swell. She knew that in fifteen minutes she would be taking a weekly history quiz. As usual, she had studied hard, but her nervousness often prevented her from getting the **A** she felt she deserved. She always seemed to panic when she took tests. Even if she really knew the material, she would begin doubting herself as soon as she saw the questions.

Susan also felt nervous when she had to take a test. She knew that she wasn't always prepared. When it came time to answer the questions, she would try to finish as quickly as possible. She wouldn't carefully read each of the multiple choice answers, but would choose the first answer that seemed to make some sense. She always breathed a sigh of relief when she got to the end of the test and could finally hand in her paper.

Tests used to scare John. Although he still felt some nervousness when taking tests, John realized that to do well he had to remain calm. While the test was being handed out, he would close his eyes and breathe deeply three times. This helped to relax him. He would then remind himself that he had studied and had used the new study methods he had learned. Realizing that he knew the material always helped build John's confidence. By the time the test was handed out, John would feel far more confident.

How Nervous Are You?

Everyone has felt nervous about a test at one time or another. But some students worry about almost every test they take. This fear, or anxiety, can cause them to do poorly, even if they are well prepared for the test. Because they do poorly, these students will probably feel even more anxiety the next time they have to take a test.

Below you will find a checklist to help you understand how you react to tests. Complete the checklist to rate your "anxiety level."

Test-Taking Checklist

Code

0 = Never   **1** = Sometimes   **2** = Often   **3** = Always

1. I don't feel that I study properly for tests. _____

2. I begin to feel nervous several days before a test. _____

3. My nervousness increases on the day of the test. _____

4. I feel that I will do poorly on tests. _____

5. If I don't know an answer, I begin to panic. _____

6. I get confused while taking tests. _____

7. Even if I have studied, I feel unsure of my answers. _____

8. I forget information that I have studied. _____

9. While I'm taking a test, I tell myself that I don't know the answers. _____

Total Points _____

Interpreting Your Testing Style

A score of 12 or more could signal a high anxiety level. Your nervousness and confusion may be causing you to do poorly on tests. You may be convinced in advance that you will fail the test. If you have difficulty with a question, you may become so upset that you can no longer concentrate.

How can you break this cycle of fear? The first step is to be prepared for the test. Now that you are using the Active Thinking Method and the Note-Taking System, preparing for a test is much easier. You've already done a lot of the work!

Let's find out how you do on a test covering the article "The Lady Pharaoh of Egypt." You have already used the Active Thinking Method while reading the article, and you have used the Note-Taking System to guide you in taking notes. Without actually studying the material, you already know quite a bit about it. Take the test *without* any further preparation.

Before you take the test, try an experiment. Follow these steps:

1. Close your eyes for thirty seconds and take a deep breath.

2. Hold the air in your lungs for about five seconds and then slowly exhale.

3. Do this three times.

4. Keep your eyes closed for another thirty seconds.

5. Remind yourself that by using the Active Thinking Method and the Note-Taking System, you have already started to study the material.

Because you have used the Active Thinking Method, you understand the material. Because you have used the Note-Taking System, you have identified the important information. You're now ready to show what you know!

Sample Test

1. When did the Lady Pharaoh of Egypt live?

    a. in the 18th century
    b. during the first century
    c. thirty-five hundred years ago
    d. 1066 A.D.

2. Thutmose I, Hatshepsut's father, was worried about

    a. providing a strong leader to rule Egypt after his death
    b. finding a new wife
    c. paying for his travels throughout Egypt
    d. finding someone to marry his daughter

3. Thutmose I wanted ＿＿＿＿＿＿ to be ruler of Egypt.

    a. Thutmose II
    b. Hatshepsut
    c. his wife
    d. Thutmose III

4. When Thutmose I died, Hatshepsut discovered that she didn't have enough power to rule alone and was forced to

    a. give up the throne
    b. plot to overthrow the government
    c. marry her half brother Thutmose II
    d. choose the next Pharaoh

5. What happened in Nubia?

    a. The people of that country refused to trade with Egypt.
    b. There was an uprising which Hatshepsut crushed.
    c. The Egyptian army was defeated by the rebels.
    d. Hatshepsut built monuments there.

6. When Thutmose II died,

    a. Thutmose III immediately became Pharaoh
    b. war broke out
    c. the people elected a new Pharaoh
    d. Hatshepsut had herself declared Pharaoh

7. During Hatshepsut's reign,

    a. the country became very poor
    b. there were many wars
    c. many monuments were built
    d. the people became unhappy

8. An obelisk is a

    a. huge, four-sided stone pillar
    b. mortuary temple
    c. type of spear
    d. gold piece of jewelry

9. Hatshepsut wanted to send an expedition to Punt because

    a. the people there were revolting against Egypt
    b. her ancestors had always hated the people of that country
    c. her navy needed something to do
    d. she wanted to trade with that country

10. Thutmose III

    a. never wanted to become Pharaoh
    b. plotted to overthrow Hatshepsut
    c. was a feebleminded ruler
    d. wanted his mother to be Pharaoh

11. Hatshepsut's decline began when

    a. Thutmose III and the priests plotted to undermine her
    b. she became too old
    c. the people became unhappy with her
    d. she began constructing monuments to herself

12. Thutmose III and the priests made it appear that

    a. Hatshepsut had built the monuments for the wrong reasons
    b. Hatshepsut was a goddess
    c. the statue of a god had chosen Thutmose III to rule
    d. Hatshepsut was not sufficiently religious

Answers

1. c	5. b	9. d
2. a	6. d	10. b
3. b	7. c	11. a
4. c	8. a	12. c

Discovering How Smart You Are

Are you surprised at how well you did on this test? You shouldn't be. Without knowing it, you have already done a lot of the work involved in studying for a test. The Active Thinking Method and the Note-Taking System have helped you learn much of the basic material. They form a solid foundation for further preparation. Of course, memorizing key facts and reviewing important concepts are also an essential part of studying for tests.

If you didn't do well on this test, do a little detective work to find out why. Perhaps you didn't read the questions and answers carefully. Perhaps you worked too quickly as you read the article or when you took notes. Look back in the article to find the correct answers to the questions you missed. Once you discover why you missed certain questions, you will know how to avoid those same mistakes in the future.

Different Types of Tests

Teachers use many different types of tests to determine how much information you understand and remember. The multiple-choice test, which you have just practiced, is one of the most common. Several other types of tests are described below.

Short Answer Tests

Question: Tell why Hatshepsut ordered an expedition to Punt.

After having used the Active Thinking Method and the Note-Taking System, you should be able to answer this question in a sentence or two.

Answer: Hatshepsut ordered an expedition to Punt because she wanted to reopen the trade routes.

True/False Tests

Question: Hatshepsut wanted to share power with her husband Thutmose II.

True   False

Answer: False

Essay Tests

Question: Describe how Thutmose II undermined Hatshepsut's rule.

Answer: Thutmose III and the priests plotted to overthrow Hatshepsut. During a religious ceremony the priests were carrying the statue of a god. The statue stopped suddenly in front of Thutmose and seemed to bow before him. The priests said that the god had chosen Thutmose to be their ruler.

Although you haven't studied the material in the article "The Lady Pharaoh of Egypt," you probably could have answered all three of these sample questions simply because you used the Active Thinking Method and the Note-Taking System. The Active Thinking Method and the Note-Taking System will help you prepare for all types of tests.

Building Confidence

Three Basic Steps for Test Preparation

1. Use the Active Thinking Method to help you understand and remember the material as you read it.

2. Use the Note-Taking System to help you identify, organize, and remember important information.

3. Review your notes several times before the test.

Four Basic Steps for Reducing Test Anxiety

1. Close your eyes before you begin the test.

2. Take a deep breath and hold it for five seconds. Slowly let out the air. Do this three times.

3. After the third breath, keep your eyes closed and remind yourself that you are well prepared for the exam.

4. Imagine the teacher handing back your test with a good grade on it.

People become confident about doing something when they have had some success at it. When you begin to do well on tests, your confidence will improve.

The three basic steps for test preparation will make your studying easier. The four basic steps for reducing test anxiety will help you remain calm when you take a test. As you practice the steps, you should find that you are doing better on tests and that you are becoming more self-confident.

On the next page you will find an optional experiment. The experiment involves reviewing your notes on the article "Newgrange—An Example of Ancient Science" and then taking a test on the material. You do not need to do this experiment if you do not want to. However, it might be valuable for you to see once again how much progress you have made. The decision to do Experiment 3 is yours.

Experiment 3   Quickly reread the article "Newgrange—An Example of Ancient Science" on page 51. Then spend approximately five minutes reviewing your notes. Then take the following test.

Test

1. Ancient people were always primitive.

   True   False

2. Newgrange was

   a. a burial mound
   b. a town in Ireland
   c. a building
   d. an ancient civilization

3. Newgrange was built

   a. about four hundred years ago
   b. about 2500 B.C.
   c. in the first century
   d. in the Middle Ages

4. Corbeling was used to

   a. bury the dead
   b. glue the stones together
   c. keep the chamber dry
   d. create calendars

5. The hole above the door was used to indicate the longest day of the year.

   True   False

6. The capstone

   a. formed the roof of the chamber
   b. was a calendar
   c. was a chamber in the mound
   d. was the captain of a ship

7. The ancient people who built Newgrange had an understanding of astronomy.

   True   False

8. Archeologists

   a. help build monuments
   b. study astronomy
   c. study ancient civilizations
   d. help solve construction problems

9. The calendar that the ancient people of Ireland used was written on the wall of Newgrange's inner chamber.

True   False

10. The passageway leads to the center of the mound.

True   False

11. How is Newgrange an example of ancient science?

_____

_____

_____

_____

_____

_____

_____

Answers

11. Newgrange is an example of ancient science because it was planned and built in such a way that the interior has remained dry for thousands of years. Newgrange also served as a simple calendar for the ancient people of Ireland. These people were able to use their knowledge of engineering and astronomy to build this monument.*

1. False	**6.** a
2. a	**7.** True
3. b	**8.** c
4. c	**9.** False
5. False	**10.** True

*Although the wording of your essay answer may be somewhat different, your answer will still be correct if it contains the same basic information and if you have communicated the information clearly.

What You Have Learned in This Chapter:

1. Three steps for test preparation

2. Four steps for reducing test anxiety

CHAPTER 10
Putting It All Together

Time Required: Approximately 90 Minutes

In this chapter you will practice using
the Active Thinking Method
and the Note-Taking System.

The Final Rehearsal

The cast had put in seven intense weeks rehearsing for the play. At first everybody was terrible. Some people forgot their lines. Others forgot where to go on stage or when to make their entrances or exits. Ms. Dunton, the drama teacher, was patient, but she was also demanding. She would not accept less than one hundred percent effort from her actors. Scenes were rehearsed again and again until they were perfect.

At first Tyrone felt that he would never be able to please the director. He had never acted before, and it had taken a lot of courage for him to try out.

Although he didn't have a major part in the play, Tyrone felt a lot of pressure. Memorizing lines was not easy for him. Fortunately, his friend Josh was able to help him develop a memory system for learning his lines. With the help of Josh's memory system and with lots of practice, Tyrone became more and more competent and confident.

The dress rehearsal was scheduled for the evening before opening night. Everyone was nervous! Ms. Dunton assured the cast that they would do fine. She reminded them that the heavy-duty work had already been done and that the dress rehearsal was just a final tune-up. And she was right! The dress rehearsal went smoothly, and the play was a smashing success. Tyrone enjoyed acting so much that he decided to try out for a lead part the following year.

Practicing New Skills

Practice is essential to the mastery of all new skills. Because we tend to become very involved in the process of learning a new skill, we often lose sight of how much improvement we are making. A final "rehearsal" can not only help us polish the rough edges off our performance, but it also can help us appreciate our improvement.

This chapter will be your final rehearsal of the Active Thinking Method and the Note-Taking System. It will help you appreciate how much smarter you've become and will also help you polish the rough edges from your new study skills. With one final dress rehearsal, you can make *Getting Smarter* a smashing success for you!

Studying a Typical Chapter in a High School Textbook

Using the Active Thinking Method, carefully read the article "Winning the Battle Against Hungry Insects," which begins below. The difficult words are not followed by stars, but they are in the glossary. Notice that no space has been provided next to the article. Now that you know how to use the method, you are no longer expected to write down your questions and answers. As you read the article, you should be able to ask yourself the questions mentally or aloud and answer them in the same way.

Because you no longer need to write down the questions and answers, preparing the chapter should require less time. *It is important, however, not to fall back into the habit of reading without actively thinking.* If you choose, you may continue writing out the questions and the answers to make sure that you are actively thinking about and remembering the material.

Read the article again and take notes using the Note-Taking System.

Finally, surprise yourself with how much smarter you have become by taking the test at the end of the chapter.

WINNING THE BATTLE AGAINST HUNGRY INSECTS

Every year millions of dollars' worth of crops are destroyed by insects. Some insects eat plants completely. Others spread diseases among plants and in so doing weaken and stunt their growth. Because insects pose such a serious threat to our food resources, farmers and scientists must wage a constant battle against them.

Not all insects, however, pose a threat to agriculture. Many insects actually help humans. Praying mantises and spiders, for example, eat other insects. Bees pollinate flowers and crops. Without such beneficial insects, human life might not be possible.

While helpful insects must be protected, those that pose a threat to the food supply must be controlled. There is quite a bit of controversy about how best to achieve these goals.

Methods for Controlling Insects

There are two major methods for controlling insects: chemical controls and biological controls. Each method has benefits and drawbacks.

Chemical Controls

Insecticides, or pesticides, are poisons which are manufactured to control insects. They are produced in spray, powder, or gas form.

Pesticides kill insects. Some are absorbed by the plant through its roots so that the entire plant becomes poisonous. Other pesticides coat the plant with a poison. When the insects eat the plant, they also eat the poison.

Disadvantages of Chemical Controls

There are six main disadvantages to using pesticides. The first involves the residue that is left on or in the edible plant. When a plant is sprayed with a pesticide, some of the pesticide evaporates or is washed away. The part that is left is called the residue and may be poisonous to humans as well as insects. This residue contains much of the poison from the pesticide. In order to make the plant safe to eat, the poison must break down, or decompose, into a nonharmful form. Because of this danger, the timing of the pesticide's application is crucial. Pesticides cannot be applied right before the harvest, or the chemical may still be toxic, or poisonous, to the people who eat the plant.

The second disadvantage to using pesticides involves the application of the poison. Pesticides must be applied evenly, so that no one plant receives too much or too little of the chemical. The process of applying the pesticide may require sophisticated equipment. Because chemicals can react with each other to form new chemicals, it is often advisable to apply only one pesticide at a time. Certain pesticides are effective only at a particular stage of an insect's growth. Thus, the timing of the application can be critical. If the chemical is not applied at the right time, the insect may not be harmed.

A third disadvantage of pesticides is that they can harm or kill the very plants they were designed to protect. This hurts farmers by reducing crop yield (the amount of crop available to be harvested). Pesticides can also spoil the appearance of the crop.

A fourth disadvantage to using pesticides is that insects can develop resistance to them. If this happens, it becomes necessary to apply stronger and stronger doses of the pesticide to maintain the same effect.

Insects can develop resistance to a pesticide very quickly because they begin reproducing when they are only a few weeks old. A new generation often appears once every few weeks. Some insects in each generation change, or mutate, slightly until a certain number of them are no longer affected by the chemicals. Those insects which do not mutate will be killed by the chemicals. Only those that do mutate will survive. Their offspring will be even more resistant to the insecticide. Thus, pesticides that are deadly to insects when they are first used will often become less toxic over a period of years.

An example that shows how insects develop resistance to a poison involves DDT. This is a very poisonous insecticide that was once used against all kinds of insects. When DDT was first developed in the 1940s, scientists thought that they had finally found a poison that could control insects once and for all. After a few years of extensive use, these scientists found that they had been wrong. A new breed of "super" insects had evolved. These insects had developed a resistance to DDT. Scientists now realize that insecticides can only be used for a limited time before insects become resistant to them.

The fifth disadvantage to using pesticides is that they can disturb the balance of nature. Pesticides cannot distinguish between harmful insects and their natural enemies—the insects which eat harmful insects and keep their numbers in check. Thus, when pesticides are used, these "friendly" insects may also be destroyed. Free from their natural enemies, harmful insects can recover and flourish in even greater numbers than before—a phenomenon known as flareback. The result is that a bigger dose of the pesticide must be used in the second round, making the imbalance even worse, and so on.

The last and most significant problem with pesticides is pollution. Pesticide residues remaining in the soil after the harvest are absorbed by the next crop. These residues can also pass into the water supply where they can be absorbed by fish, animals, and even people.

Although scientists do not fully understand the long-term effects of chemicals on people, many studies have proven that pesticides can cause damage to the genes in animal cells. When genetic damage occurs, future generations may be born with defects or abnormalities. Pesticides can also poison people who manufacture, handle, and apply the chemicals. This is especially true when pesticides are breathed or come into contact with the skin.

Advantages of Chemical Controls

There are three advantages to using pesticides. The main one is that they are effective. Pesticides kill bugs! A second is that pesticides are reliable; when farmers use them, they can generally be sure that insect pests will be controlled. The third advantage is time; pesticides can be applied fast, so that harmful insects are destroyed fast.

Biological Controls

Insects can also be controlled by biological means. There are five major methods of biological control.

Predators (birds, toads, and spiders and beneficial insects like ladybugs and praying mantises) eat the harmful insects, thus balancing out the damage done by them. In some instances, beneficial insects can be bred and released in an area to control a specific harmful insect. Such a form of control requires cooperation. If one farmer or gardener tries to use predators to control unwanted insects, and a neighbor sprays pesticides, the helpful insects may be destroyed.

A second method involves using diseases to control insects. Bacterial or viral diseases which harm only certain insects can be released in an area. The disease will attack only those insects without harming other insects or plants.

The technique of sterilizing male insects is a third form of biological control. In this method, harmful insects are raised in a laboratory and then exposed to radiation. The radiation makes them sterile (not able to produce offspring). The sterile males are then released in a certain area to mate with the females. Because the males have been sterilized, the eggs laid by the females will never hatch. Thus, the population slowly decreases. The main drawback to this technique is that sometimes a few of the males who have received radiation do not become sterile. These males mate with females and add to the number of harmful insects instead of decreasing it. Another drawback is that this method is costly. It also takes a lot of time before the population of a particular insect is reduced.

A fourth method of biological control is to develop crops that can resist insect attacks. Scientists do this by finding and breeding individual plants which show an unusual resistance to the attack of particular insects. However, the process is complex and may take years to complete.

Mixed planting is a fifth method of biologically controlling insects. This method involves planting a few kinds of crops together instead of just one kind. If the field is attacked by insects which eat one kind of plant, only some of the plants will be affected.

Disadvantages of Biological Controls

There are four disadvantages of biological controls. The main one is that, used alone, they are not as effective as chemical controls. They are also less reliable. These kinds of controls can be difficult to use. For example, to use predators to control harmful insects, scientists must first raise friendly insects and then release them in the fields. Finally, they can be time consuming. Using sterilized male insects is an example of a method which requires time.

Advantages of Biological Controls

The main advantage to using biological controls is that they are less harmful to people, plants, animals, and the environment. Many people feel that the effectiveness of insecticides is outweighed by the harm they can cause. Generally, biological controls are less expensive than chemical controls. Finally, when a few of these kinds of controls are used at the same time, their effectiveness is increased. As more and more scientific research is applied to biological controls, even greater effectiveness is possible.

Integrated Control

How, then, is the battle against hungry insects won? Which method of control, chemical or biological, is more effective? The answer may be to use both methods at the same time. This is called integrated control.

The goal with integrated control is not to destroy *all* harmful insects, as it is with chemical control. Rather, the goal is to keep harmful insect populations below the level at which they cause farmers to lose money. Since there is so much concern today about the harmful effects of pesticides on the environment, biological controls are preferred to chemical controls. Insecticides, however, when used with care, can play an important role in integrated control.

The battle against hungry insects will never be won completely. There will always be harmful insects. Integrated control provides a way to keep harmful insects from causing major damage to crops, without harming our health or the safety of the environment.

Sample Questions and Answers

Now that you have read the material, it is time to compare your questions and answers with the sample questions and answers below. Although you probably asked and answered your questions mentally, it will be good practice for you to compare them with those below. As you review them, you will need to look back at each section of the article.

Question: How can we win the battle against hungry insects? (Since this question comes from the main title, it can't be answered until the entire article has been read. See the end of this section for the answer.)

Question: What are the methods for controlling insects?

Answer: There are two main methods: chemical controls and biological controls.

Question: What are chemical controls?

Answer: Chemical controls are insecticides or pesticides; these are poisons which kill insects.

Question: What are the disadvantages of pesticides?

Answer: There are six disadvantages of pesticides:

1. The residue that is left can be poisonous.
2. The application can be difficult.
3. Pesticides can harm the plants they were designed to protect.
4. Insects can develop a resistance to the pesticides.
5. Chemicals can disturb the balance of nature.
6. Pesticides pollute.

Question: What are the advantages of pesticides?

Answer: There are three advantages of pesticides:

1. They are effective.
2. They are relatively reliable.
3. They can be applied fast, and they work fast.

Question: What are biological controls?

Answer: Biological controls are ways of fighting insects without using chemicals. There are five main methods:

1. Releasing natural predators
2. Releasing diseases which harm only specific insects
3. Sterilizing male insects
4. Breeding resistant crops
5. Mixed planting

Question: What are the disadvantages of biological controls?

Answer: There are four disadvantages:

1. They are generally less effective than chemical controls.
2. They are less reliable.
3. They are more difficult to use than chemicals.
4. They generally take more time to be effective.

Question: What are the advantages of biological controls?

Answer: There are three advantages:

1. They are nontoxic to people and don't harm the environment.
2. They are less expensive than chemical controls.
3. They can be effective when a few kinds are used at the same time.

Question: What is integrated control?

Answer: Integrated control is using biological and chemical methods at the same time in order to control insects.

Question: (from the main title) How can we win the battle against hungry insects?

Answer: We can never win the battle against hungry insects completely. But by using integrated control, we can keep harmful insect populations low without harming ourselves or our environment.

Congratulations!

You have completed your "dress rehearsal" of the Active Thinking Method. With practice, this system will become second nature to you. You will find yourself asking questions and answering them as you read. The result will be greater comprehension and retention of the material.

Now take notes on this article using the three steps in the Note-Taking Method. Remember to include:

1. Main Ideas
2. Details
3. Point

Comparing Your Notes

Here are sample notes that have been taken from the article "Winning the Battle Against Hungry Insects." Compare your notes with these. Yours should be almost the same. If they are not, make the necessary corrections in your notes. Look back in the article when necessary.

Winning the Battle Against Hungry Insects

Crops destroyed by insects—millions of $ lost

Some insects helpful

Controversy over how to control harmful insects

Methods for Controlling Insects

- 2 methods—chemical and biological
- each has benefits and drawbacks

Chemical Controls

insecticides or pesticides—spray, powder, or gas

- kill bugs
- some chemicals absorbed by plant
- some coat plant w/poison

Disadvantages of Chemical Controls

1. Residue—left on or in plant

   - poisonous
   - must break down before plant is eaten
   - timing of application important—can't be done right before harvest

2. Difficulty applying

   - need machinery to apply evenly
   - chemicals react with each other, so only 1 pesticide can be applied at a time
   - pesticide effective at particular stage of insect's growth—timing important

3. Harmful effects

   - injure plants
   - reduce yield (amount of crop available to be harvested)
   - spoil appearance
   - can destroy plants

4. Insect resistance

   - more and more insecticides needed to destroy insects
   - insects become resistant to insecticides by mutation
   - resistance comes quickly because of quick reproduction
   - DDT—used in 1940s—insects developed resistance

5. Balance of nature disturbed

- beneficial insects destroyed
- more pesticides needed to compensate for loss
- flareback—harmful insects come back in greater numbers

6. Pollution

- Pest. remain in soil and pass into water supply
- animal studies show pest. cause genetic damage
- poisonous effect on people

Advantages of Chemical Controls

1. effective
2. predictable
3. fast working

Biological Controls—5 main methods

1. Predators (birds, toads, ladybugs, praying mantises, spiders)

- need cooperation among neighbors, or one farmer's pesticides may kill another's beneficial insects

2. Diseases

- specific bacterial or viral diseases will kill only specific insects

3. Sterilizing male insects

- radiation makes males sterile
- sterile males released to mate w/females
- females lay eggs that don't hatch
- insect population reduced
- drawbacks
  some males don't become sterile
  costly
  takes time

4. Developing resistant crops

- crops resistant to insect attacks
- bred from unusually resistant individuals
- complex
- may take years

5. Mixed planting

- several kinds of crops planted together
- insects will attack only a portion of field

Disadvantages of Biological Control

1. not as effective
2. less reliable
3. more difficult to use
4. more time consuming

Advantages of Biological Controls

1. nontoxic
2. less expensive than chemical controls
3. more effective when several biological controls used together

Integrated Control

biological and chemical controls used together

Point

There are two main methods for controlling insects: chemical controls and biological controls. Each method has its advantages and disadvantages. Integrated control, using both biological and chemical means, seems to be the most effective way to wage the battle against hungry insects.

Showing What You Know

Although you haven't actually studied the material in this article, you already know a lot about it. You've read the article using the Active Thinking Method, and you've used the Note-Taking Method with the material. You can prove to yourself just how much you've learned by taking the following test.

True/False

1. Pesticides can be absorbed by plants through their roots.

   True   False

2. DDT is as effective today against insects as it was when it was first used.

   True   False

3. There is no proof that pesticides can cause genetic damage.

   True   False

4. It isn't important when pesticides are applied.

   True   False

5. Bacterial diseases can be used intentionally to control insects.

   True   False

6. Biological controls used singly are not as effective as chemical controls.

   True   False

7. People can be exposed to pesticides when they eat plants.

   True   False

8. Some insects are good for plants.

   True   False

9. Farmers try to help insects develop resistance to chemicals.

   True   False

10. Insect predators are the most effective means of controlling insects.

    True   False

Multiple Choice

11. Insects

    a. breed slowly
    b. pollute the soil after the harvest
    c. can develop resistance to pesticides
    d. never kill each other

12. A pesticide

    a. kills insects
    b. controls the insect's growth
    c. drives the insect away with its bad smell or taste
    d. blinds the insect

13. The technique of sterilizing male insects

    a. is always effective
    b. is a quick means of controlling insects
    c. involves exposing male insects to radiation
    d. both a and b

14. A disadvantage to using pesticides is

    a. the pollution pesticides cause
    b. the harmful residue left on the plant
    c. the difficulty of application
    d. all of the above

15. An important advantage to biological controls is

    a. the saving of time
    b. the avoidance of pollution and danger to humans
    c. the saving of money
    d. that most farmers prefer this method

Comparing Your Answers

1. T	6. T	11. c
2. F	7. T	12. a
3. F	8. T	13. c
4. F	9. F	14. d
5. T	10. F	15. b

Give yourself one point for each correct answer. If you scored above 11 on this test, then you understand and remember the information. If you scored 11 or below on this test, then you need to take more time as you read and take notes. Writing out the questions and the answers when using the Active Thinking Method may still be necessary for a while.

You are on your own now. You know how to read information and how to take notes so that you can understand and remember what you have read.

CHAPTER 11
Final Evaluation: What You Have Learned

Time Required: Approximately 10 Minutes

In this chapter you will find out how
much you have learned by using this book.

Being Intelligent *and* Being Smart

At the very beginning of this book there was a "Message to Students." The message began: "Being intelligent is not the same as being smart." The message went on to say:

> . . . being smart requires more than intelligence. Being smart involves being practical and having common sense, too. Being intelligent may be knowing a lot of facts that will help to answer homework questions, but being smart is remembering to take home the books you need to do the homework. Being smart is knowing *what* to study for an exam and knowing *how* to study for that exam efficiently. Being smart is figuring out how to complete a long assignment within a reasonable amount of time and do a good job on it without having to give up large parts of your life.

You have just completed a book whose purpose has been to teach you how to get smarter. It's time for you to find out just how much you have learned. Here are two final checklists. Look at the codes and then place the appropriate number after each question on the checklists.

Study Habits Checklist

Code
0 = Never   **1** = Rarely   **2** = Sometimes   **3** = Often   **4** = Always

1. I set priorities when I study.   _____

2. I set academic goals for myself.   _____

3. I have the proper supplies available when I
   study.   _____

4. I have a system for writing down and
   organizing my assignments.   _____

5. I use memory techniques to help me
   remember.   _____

6. I study under good conditions at home.   _____

7. I have found a good place for studying while at
   school.   _____

8. I take only a ten- to fifteen-minute break
   between study sessions.   _____

9. I study without a lot of distractions.   _____

10. I use a schedule to plan my time.   _____

Total Points   _____

Any score greater than 30 indicates that you have mastered good study habits. The higher your score, the more organized you are and the better prepared you will be.

If your score is below 30, we suggest that you review the section in the book that covers the area in which your score is low. You can easily find the section by looking in the Table of Contents.

A score of 40 would be ideal. Such a score would indicate that you are very organized. If you want to aim for a score of 40, concentrate on improving your performance in the particular area in which your score was lower than you wish.

Study Skills Checklist

Code

0 = Never   **1** = Rarely   **2** = Sometimes   **3** = Often   **4** = Always

1. I use the Active Thinking Method when I study.   _____

When I use the Active Thinking Method,

2. I first read the title.   _____

3. I then read the introduction.   _____

4. I turn the main title and each subtitle into a question.   _____

5. I read the material carefully.   _____

6. I learn the meaning of difficult words.   _____

7. I answer the questions about the subtitles and the main title.   _____

8. I use the Note-Taking System.   _____

When I use the Note-Taking System,

9. I write down the main ideas from the reading material.   _____

10. I write down the details under each main idea.   _____

11. I write down the point of the material I have studied.   _____

If I suffer a great deal of test anxiety,

12. I close my eyes before I begin the test.   _____

13. I take three deep breaths and hold each for five seconds.   _____

14. I keep my eyes closed and remind myself that I am well prepared for the exam.   _____

15. I imagine the teacher handing back my test with a good grade on it.   _____

Total Points   _____

Any score greater than 50 indicates that you have mastered good study skills. The higher your score, the better your study skills are.

If your score is below 50, we suggest that you review Chapters 5 through 10.

A score of 60 would be ideal. If you do have a score above 50, your grades should reflect your improved study skills. If you would like to achieve a higher score, concentrate on improving your performance in the areas in which your score was lower than you wish.

Glossary

archeologist: A scientist who studies ancient civilizations.

assume: To believe something to be true; take for granted.

capable: Having ability.

capstone: The top stone in a dome-shaped structure which forms the roof of that structure.

civilization: The total culture of a people, nation, period, etc.

commission: To order; to authorize.

crop yield: The amount of a crop available to be harvested.

decline: A move down to a lower rank or level.

destined: Determined in advance by fate.

diameter: The distance of a straight line going from one side of a circle, through its center, to the other side.

ebony: A dark, heavy hardwood.

excel: To do well at something.

expedition: A journey whose purpose is to explore.

gene: A chemical unit that carries characteristics from parent to child.

genetic damage: Harm done to the genes.

generation: A group of individuals born and living at the same time.

hieroglyphics: Egyptian picture writings.

illuminate: To light up.

insecticide: A poison which kills insects.

keenly: Strongly; intensely.

laden: Loaded; burdened.

monument: A building or statue which is built to show the glory of someone.

mortuary: A building where the dead are brought before burial.

mutate: To change chemically or physically (said of an organism's hereditary material).

myrrh: A precious plant used to make perfumes.

obelisk: A tall, four-sided stone pillar which comes to a point at the top.

outfit: To supply.

overthrow: To conquer.

pesticide: A poison which kills insects.

Pharaoh: The ruler of ancient Egypt.

predator: An animal or insect that hunts and kills other animals or insects.

primitive: Seeming to be uncivilized, crude, or simple.

prosperity: Wealth.

prosperous: Wealthy.

radiant: Glowing.

recede: To move back.

reign: Period during which someone rules.

residue: The remainder; the part that is left.

successor: Someone who will inherit the throne.

toxic: Poisonous.

tradition: The practices followed by a culture or religion.

undermine: To weaken.

victorious: Having won a victory.

MATERIALS NEEDED AT HOME

Paper	_____	Assignment Sheet	_____
Pens	_____	Hole Punch	_____
Pencils	_____	Watch or Clock	_____
Binder	_____	School Books	_____
Ruler	_____	Phone Number of One Student in Each Class	_____
Class Schedule	_____	_____	_____
Calculator	_____	_____	_____
Dictionary	_____	_____	_____
Pencil Sharpener	_____		

MATERIALS NEEDED AT SCHOOL

Paper	_____	Assignment Sheet	_____
Pens	_____	Hole Punch	_____
Pencils	_____	Watch or Clock	_____
Binder	_____	Completed Homework	_____
Class Schedule	_____	Gym Clothes	_____
Calculator	_____	_____	_____
Dictionary	_____	_____	_____
School Books	_____	_____	_____

MATERIALS NEEDED AT HOME

Paper	———	Assignment Sheet	———
Pens	———	Hole Punch	———
Pencils	———	Watch or Clock	———
Binder	———	School Books	———
Ruler	———	Phone Number of One Student in Each Class	———
Class Schedule	———	———————	———
Calculator	———	———————	———
Dictionary	———	———————	———
Pencil Sharpener	———		

MATERIALS NEEDED AT SCHOOL

Paper	———	Assignment Sheet	———
Pens	———	Hole Punch	———
Pencils	———	Watch or Clock	———
Binder	———	Completed Homework	———
Class Schedule	———	Gym Clothes	———
Calculator	———	———————	———
Dictionary	———	———————	———
School Books	———	———————	———

Assignment Sheet

Subjects						
Monday ___						
Tuesday ___						
Wednesday ___						
Thursday ___						
Friday ___						
Date of Next Test						
Next Report Due						